WENFORD BRIDGE TO FOWEY

Vic Mitchell and Keith Smith

 Middleton Press

Cover picture: The branch train from Lostwithiel was recorded at Fowey on 21st June 1956. 0-4-2T no. 1408 was normally based at Plymouth Laira Shed and was on loan to St.Blazey. This was the only Cornish branch on which this class worked regularly. (H.Davies)

Published February 1998

ISBN 1 901706 09 5

© *Middleton Press, 1998*

Design Deborah Goodridge

Published by
    Middleton Press
    Easebourne Lane
    Midhurst, West Sussex
    GU29 9AZ
Tel: 01730 813169
Fax: 01730 812601

Printed & bound by Biddles Ltd,
    Guildford and Kings Lynn

CONTENTS

35	Bodmin General	84	Golant Halt
54	Bodmin Parkway	66	Lostwithiel
24	Boscarne Junction	120	St.Blazey
20	Dunmere Junction	6	Wenford
102	Fowey	1	Wenford Bridge
88	Fowey Jetties		

ACKNOWLEDGEMENTS

In addition to those mentioned in the photographic credits, we would like to thank the following for all the assistance received: J.Barry, N.L.Browne, D.Cullum, F.Hornby, I.Nisbet, J.S.Petley, H.Phillips, R.Ruffell, Mr D. & Dr S. Salter, B.Shadwick, N.Sprinks, G.Stacey, R.Webster, E.Youldon and, as always, our wives.

GEOGRAPHICAL SETTING

Wenford is situated on the western edge of Bodmin Moor, a Granite mass which has been worked for its stone and the product of its breakdown - china clay. The route descends the narrow valley of the River Camel to Boscarne Junction from where, after reversal, it climbs steeply around The Beacon to reach Bodmin (General). The small county town is close to the watershed between the Camel and Fowey valleys. The remainder of the route follows the latter to the coast at Fowey (pronounced FOY, like boy), where a natural deep water anchorage is available on the western bank, about one mile inland.

The entire area is formed predominantly of Old Red Sandstone and it was through this material that the Fowey - St.Blazey line had to pass in a tunnel at the summit of its steep gradients. The bore is the longest in Cornwall.

The maps are to the scale of 25 ins to 1 mile, except where otherwise shown, and the gradient profiles are near picture nos 6, 26, 36, 65, 81 and 120.

North is at the top of the maps and diagrams, unless a bold arrow indicates otherwise.

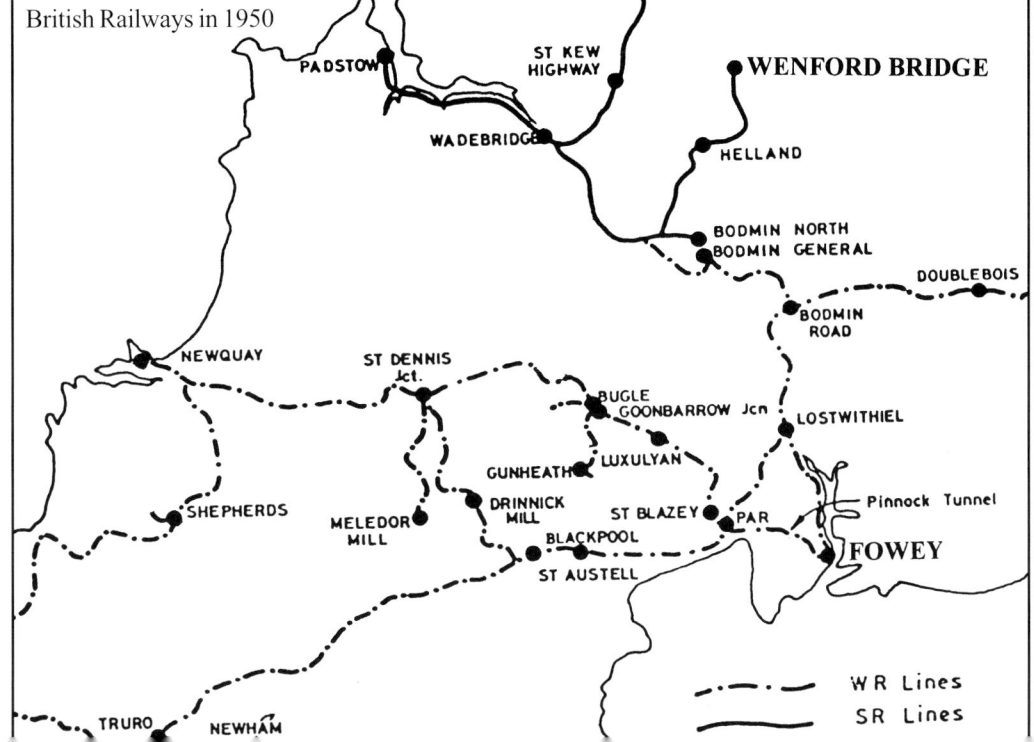

HISTORICAL BACKGROUND

Wenford Bridge - Boscarne Junction

The passenger line of the Bodmin & Wadebridge Railway between these towns was opened on 4th July 1834, the goods line to Wenford Bridge following on 30th September of that year. The London & South Western Railway took control of the lines in 1847 and absorbed the company in 1886, but it was not until 1895 that the systems were connected together by the North Cornwall Line. They became part of the Southern Railway in 1923.

Boscarne Junction - Bodmin General

This section was opened to all traffic by the Great Western Railway on 3rd September 1888 and allowed Wenford clay to be conveyed to ports other than Padstow.

Bodmin General - Bodmin Road

The GWR brought this branch into use on 27th May 1887. Like the lines mentioned above, it was built to standard gauge. Transhipment to broad gauge at Bodmin Road was necessary until 1892.

Bodmin Road - Lostwithiel

This was part of the broad gauge Cornwall Railway which was opened between Plymouth and Truro to passengers on 4th May 1859 and for goods on 10th October of that year. It became part of the GWR in 1876 and was converted to standard gauge in 1892.

Lostwithiel - Fowey

The Lostwithiel & Fowey Railway opened for the conveyance of minerals to wharves at Carne Point on 1st June 1869 and was of broad gauge. Financial problems caused its closure from 1880 until 1895, when it was acquired by the GWR and relaid to standard gauge. It was extended a short distance to Fowey and opened to all traffic on 16th September 1895. There were temporary closures during both World Wars owing to restrictions on coastal shipping and military occupation of the area.

Fowey - St. Blazey

This section formed the southern part of the Cornwall Minerals Railway and was opened on 1st June 1874, for freight only. A passenger service began on 20th June 1876 and the line was taken over by the GWR in the following year.

Recent history

Closures	Passengers	All traffic
Wenford Bridge - Boscarne Jn.	Never open	3.10.1983
Boscarne Jn. - Bodmin Gen.	30.1.1967	3.10.1983
Bodmin Gen. - Bodmin Road	30.1.1967	3.10.1983
Bodmin Rd. - Lostwithiel	Open	Open
Lostwithiel - Fowey	4.1.1965	Open for clay
Fowey - St. Blazey	31.12.1934	1.7.1968

Nationalisation on 1st January 1948 resulted in the area forming part of the Western Region of British Railways but the Wenford branch became part of the Southern Region. It was transferred to the Western Region on 1st January 1963. Bodmin Road was renamed Bodmin Parkway on 4th November 1983.

The Bodmin Railway Preservation Society was formed in 1984 and the Bodmin & Wenford Railway plc issued shares in 1985 to enable the Bodmin Parkway-Boscarne Junction section to be purchased, complete with track. A Light Railway Order was obtained on 31st August 1989 and short trips from Bodmin General commenced. Regular services to Bodmin Parkway were restored on 17th June 1990 and trains started to run to Boscarne Junction again on 14th August 1996.

Privatisation of BR in 1995-96 resulted in passenger services being provided by the Great Western Trains Co. and by (South) Wales & West Railway. Freight trains eventually became the responsibility of English Welsh & Scottish Railways, as did most sidings. Main lines, loops and signalling were transferred to Railtrack.

PASSENGER SERVICES

Details of local trains in the Bodmin area are contained in our *Branch Lines around Bodmin* and main line services will be outlined in a future volume. The Wenford Bridge to Boscarne Junction section has never appeared in a passenger timetable, but tickets were issued at Wadebridge permitting travel in a brake van.

St. Blazey - Fowey

This route provided the only service to Fowey between 1876 and 1895, passengers from the main line having to change both at Par and St. Blazey in most cases. There were 4 or 5 trains each weekday until 1891, the figures increasing to eight thereafter and rising to ten in 1895. By 1903, it had dropped to six and tailed off to three when services ceased to be advertised after St. Blazey station closed on 21st September 1925. However, workmen were recorded as being carried until 31st December 1934.

Lostwithiel - Fowey

The timetables for selected years showed trains (weekdays only) thus:

Year	Trains
1895	3
1905	3
1913	7
1924	7
1928	11
1938	12
1943	10
1948	11
1958	8
1964	9

There were two extra trips on Saturdays in 1948 and five extra in the 1958 timetable.

There were a few return trips on the branch on some Sundays in the Summers of 1994-95, organised by Lostwithiel Town Council, but the trains turned back at the end of BR property.

July 1878

December 1895
July 1924

The 1 inch to 1 mile map of 1946 shows De Lank Quarries and Wenfordbridge top right and Bodmin Road lower right. The remainder of the route to Fowey is on the next map. The SR station is near the centre of Bodmin; it was termed Bodmin North from 1949 until closure in 1967.

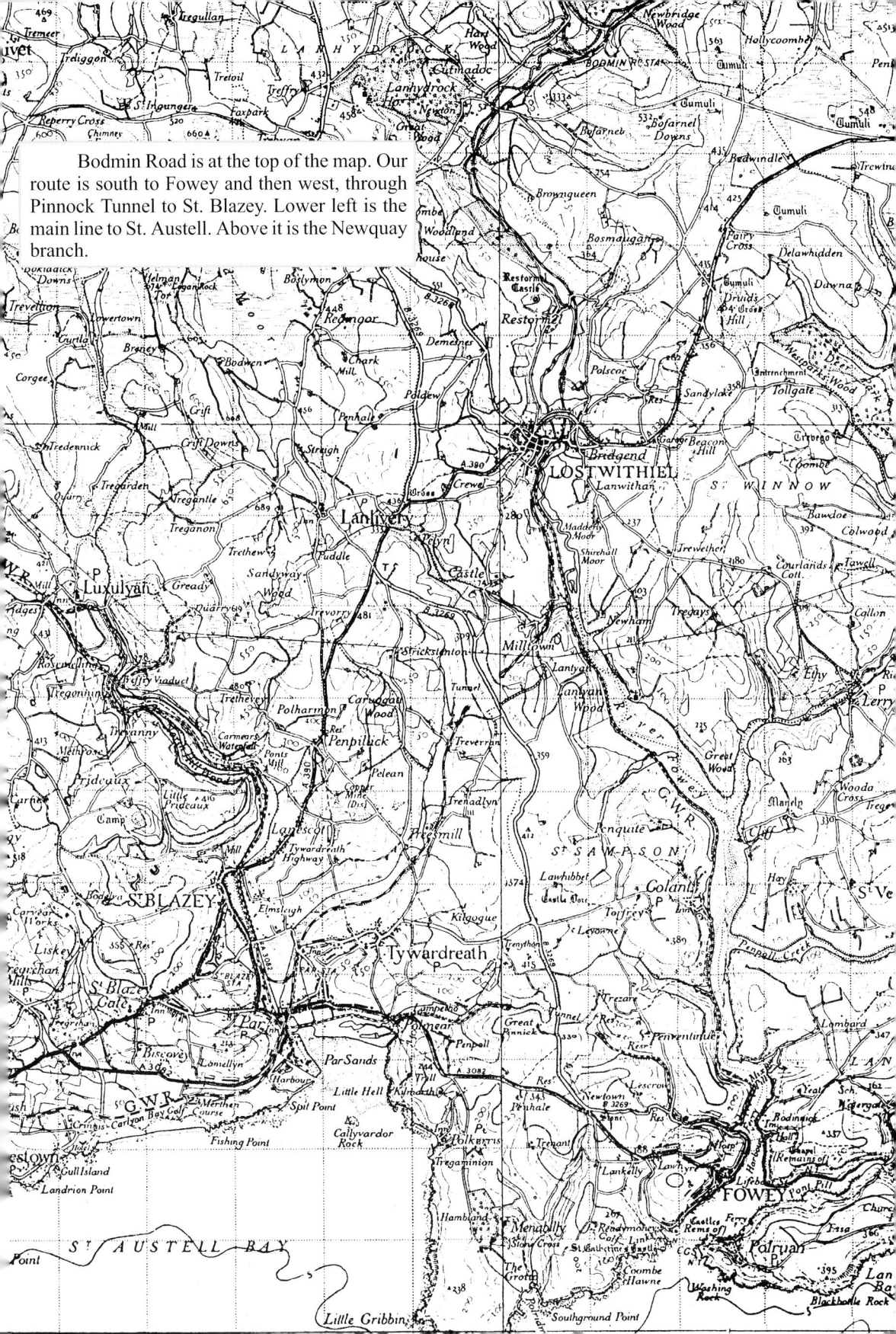

Bodmin Road is at the top of the map. Our route is south to Fowey and then west, through Pinnock Tunnel to St. Blazey. Lower left is the main line to St. Austell. Above it is the Newquay branch.

WENFORD BRIDGE

1. The two sidings terminated beyond the right edge of this southward view. The chimneys of Wenford Clay Dries are in the distance and the connection to De Lank Quarries is in the foreground. (R.C.Riley)

De Lank Quarries (T. W. Ward) siding. - The siding crosses a roadway immediately outside the Company's boundary, the route thence being by a steep incline to the De Lank Quarries, the gradient of which is 1 in 8 rising to the quarries.

The points farthest away from Wenford connecting with No. 1 catch siding are fitted with a spring lever and lie normally for No. 1 catch siding. The points leading to No. 3 catch siding (nearest Wenford) must lie normally for that siding and must be secured in that position by a padlock, the key of which is kept in the goods office at Wenford Bridge terminus.

The Company's engine must not proceed on to the siding beyond the Company's boundary. Outgoing wagons, after being moved by hand into the siding by Messrs. Ward's employees to a point between the Company's boundary and the hand points leading to the siding, must be drawn there from by the Company's engine. Ingoing wagons are berthed in the Company's middle siding, and on application by Messrs. Ward's employees are either moved by engine power or pushed by hand over the points leading to the Quarries' siding and hauled thence by the firm's horses through that siding to the incline.

Not more than two wagons must be worked either up, or down, the De Lank incline at any one time.

Before any wagons are placed upon or taken from the Company's siding leading to the private sidings, the key of the padlock securing the points leading to No. 3 catch siding will be obtained by Messrs. Ward's employees from the Goods Clerk at Wenford, who will be held responsible for satisfying himself that the exchange of wagons can be carried out with safety. He must also satisfy himself that the points leading to No. 3 catch siding are not set for the Company's sidings until trucks which have been lowered from the incline have come to rest at the foot of the incline.

The Goods Clerk will also be responsible for satisfying himself that the points are correctly set for the catch sidings, secured by padlock in that position and the key returned to him as soon as the exchange of wagons has been completed.

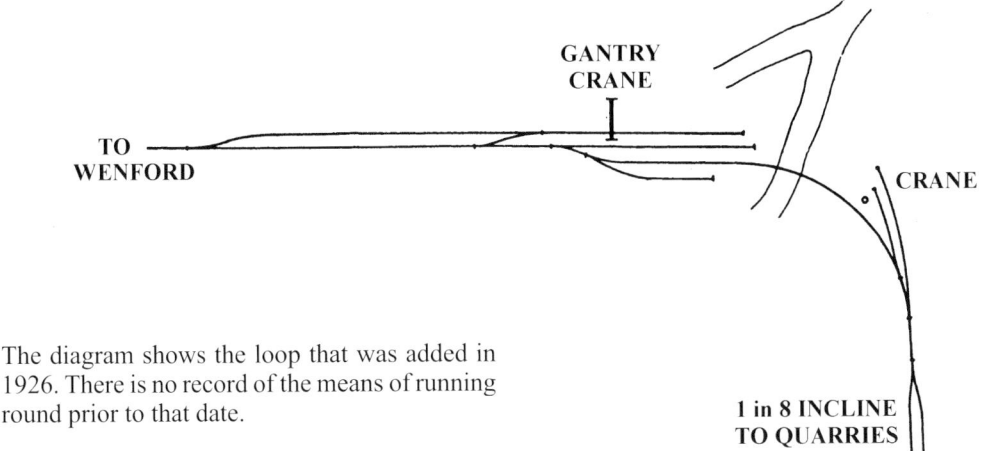

The diagram shows the loop that was added in 1926. There is no record of the means of running round prior to that date.

2. Looking east from the same point that the previous photograph was taken, we see the connection from BR on the right and the 1 in 8 rope-worked incline that once brought granite blocks down from the quarries of T.W.Ward & Sons. This 1949 photograph suggests a long period of disuse, although official closure was not until 1950. (J.H.Aston)

3. The loading gantry, erected by the SR in 1926, was of 5-ton capacity and intended mainly for the transfer of timber. Inward traffic was predominantly coal and fertiliser. The locomotive is 2-4-0WT no. 30585, now preserved at the Buckinghamshire Railway Centre. (D.Lawrence)

4. Sister locomotive no. 30587 was recorded shunting prior to detachment of its short train on 19th August 1958. This engine survives in the museum at Buckfastleigh station. A locked catch point was provided to prevent runaways. The branch was truncated in this vicinity in 1971. (A.E.Bennett)

5. The Beattie Well Tanks seen in the previous pictures dated from the 1880s and were superseded by ex-GWR Pannier Tanks in 1962. No. 1369 was photographed on the loop prior to departure on 17th August 1962. General freight traffic ceased on the branch on 1st May 1967, but closure north of Wenford (kilns) occurred on 13th February 1967. (N.D.Mundy)

WENFORD

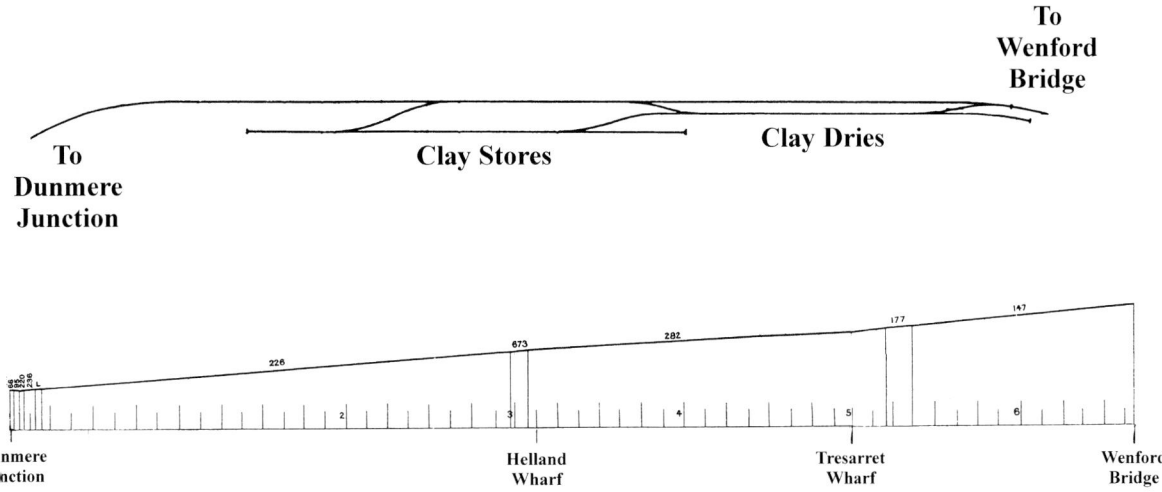

6. China clay was transported on the branch from 1862. The dries were operated by H.D.Pochin & Co. Ltd. until 1932. The pan kilns required large tonnages of coal to be brought in by rail.
(M.Dart coll.)

7. Now we can enjoy three photographs from 1954, when the remaining trio of Well Tanks were still active. The full name of the siding was then English Clays Lovering Pochin Co. Ltd., the company being a constituent of English China Clays Ltd. This is no. 30585 again. (R.M.Casserley)

Working timetable for 1940

WENFORD MINERAL LINE—WEEK-DAYS ONLY

Distance		DOWN	Q Freight arr. a.m.	Q Freight dep. a.m.	Freight arr. a.m.	Freight dep. a.m.	Q Freight arr. a.m.	Q Freight dep. a.m.
m.	c.							
—	—	Wadebridge	...	7 15	A	10 0	...	...
2	72	Grogley	...	...	...	...	...	...
4	32	Nanstallon Siding	...	...	10 12	10 20	...	...
4	62	Boscarne Junct.	7 30	8 0	10 23	10 50	...	11 40
5	07	Dunmere Junct.	8	4	10	54	11	44
5	25	Dunmere Siding	8 5	8 25	10 55	11 15	11 45	12 5
8	12	Helland Siding	...	...	11 44	11 49	12 34	12 39
9	71	Road Stone Co. & }	...	...	11 58	12 8	12 48	12 53
10	0	Parkin's Siding						
10	28	Tresarrett Siding	...	...	12 12	12 22	12 57	1 2
11	28	China Clay Co.'s Siding	9 15	...	12 27	12 47	1 7	1 17
11	63	Wenford	—	—	12 51	...	1 21	...

Distance		UP	Q Freight arr. a.m.	Q Freight dep. a.m.	Freight arr. p.m.	Freight dep. p.m.	Q arr. p.m.	Q dep. p.m.
m.	c.							
—	—	Wenford	...	...	B	1 35	...	1 45
0	35	China Clay Co.'s Siding	...	10 0	1 40	2 15	1 50	2 15
1	35	Tresarrett Siding	...	...	2 20	2 30	2 20	2 30
1	52	Road Stone Co. & }	...	...	2 34	2 45	2 34	2 45
1	72	Parkin's Siding						
3	51	Helland Siding	...	...	2 54	2 59	2 54	2 59
6	39	Dunmere Siding	10 42	10 44	3 22	3 24	3 22	3 24
6	57	Dunmere Junct.	10 45	11 5	3 25	3 45	3 25	3 45
7	01	Boscarne Junct.	11 9	...	3 49	4 13	3 49	4 13
11	63	Wadebridge	—	—	4 26	...	4 26	...

A—Will not apply when 7.15 a.m. from Wadebridge " Q " and 11.40 a.m. from Boscarne Junction " Q " run.   B—Will not apply when 10.0 a.m. from China Clay Co.'s Siding to Boscarne Junction and 1.45 p.m. Wenford to Wadebridge " Q " trains run.

8. Some of the many grades of china clay were despatched bagged in vans. In earlier days, casks had been used. Vans could be loaded on the running line providing they were not more than six in number, had handbrakes secured and were trapped by a locked wheel scotch. (H.C.Casserley)

9. The sheeting of open wagons presented many problems, this resulting in the development of hoods in the early 1970s. This view from July 1960 includes no. 30587 and a loading shelter in embryo. (H.Davies)

10. Known as "Clay Hoods", the modified wagons were quick to load and kept the clay dry. On 6th October 1982, shunting was by means of a tractor and diesel no. 08945 was undertaking the haulage. (D.Mitchell)

11. The site of the sidings remained undeveloped in 1997 and had the potential for railway use again. Vast sums of Railway Facilities Grant set aside by the Government remained unclaimed while the output went by road. (M.Turvey)

SOUTH OF WENFORD

12. When the BWR opened in 1834, the term "station" was not widely used; the maritime term "Wharf" was thus applied to stopping places. This is Tresarrett Wharf (a goods loop) in June 1960. Several of the wharfingers were women. (H.Cowan)

13. Helland Wharf was visited by the Plymouth Railway Circle's brake van special on 31st May 1958. The line was unfenced and so the Working Instructions ordered drivers to "keep a good look out" and to adhere to the 10mph speed limit on the branch. (M.Dart)

14. The same special train was recorded at the picturesque Helland Crossing. The principal traffic on the line in the early years had been "sand" from the coast. This was a mineral-rich material of sea-shell origin which was of value as a fertiliser in land improvement schemes. The wharf was behind the cottage and was in use until 2nd May 1960. (M.Daly)

WENFORD MINERAL LINE—WEEK-DAYS ONLY

Distance		DOWN	Q Freight		Freight		Q Freight	
m.	c.		arr. a.m.	dep. a.m.	arr. a.m.	dep. a.m.	arr. a.m.	dep. a.m.
—	—	Wadebridge	...	7 15	A	10 0	...	...
2	72	Grogley	...	...	...	...	...	...
4	32	Nanstallon Siding	...	...	10 12	10 20	...	...
4	62	Boscarne Junct.	7 30	8 0	10 23	10 50	...	11 40
5	07	Dunmere Junct.	8	4	10	54	11	44
5	25	Dunmere Siding	8 5	8 25	10 55	11 15	11 45	12 5
8	12	Helland Siding	...	...	11 44	11 49	12 34	12 39
9	71	Road Stone Co. &	...	...	11 58	12 8	12 48	12 53
10	0	Parkin's Siding						
10	28	Tresarrett Siding	...	...	12 12	12 22	12 57	1 2
11	28	China Clay Co.'s Siding	9 15	...	12 27	12 47	1 7	1 17
11	63	Wenford	—	—	12 51	...	1 21	...

Distance		UP	Q Freight		Freight		Q	
m.	c.		arr. a.m.	dep. a.m.	arr. p.m.	dep. p.m.	arr. p.m.	dep. p.m.
—	—	Wenford	...	...	B	1 35	...	1 45
0	35	China Clay Co.'s Siding	...	10 0	1 40	2 15	1 50	2 15
1	35	Tresarrett Siding	...	...	2 20	2 30	2 20	2 30
1	52	Road Stone Co. &	...	...	2 34	2 45	2 34	2 45
1	72	Parkin's Siding						
3	51	Helland Siding	...	...	2 54	2 59	2 54	2 59
6	39	Dunmere Siding	10 42	10 44	3 22	3 24	3 22	3 24
6	57	Dunmere Junct.	10 45	11 5	3 25	3 45	3 25	3 45
7	01	Boscarne Junct.	11 9	...	3 49	4 13	3 49	4 13
11	63	Wadebridge	...	—	4 26	...	4 26	...

A—Will not apply when 7.15 a.m. from Wadebridge " Q " and 11.40 a.m. from Boscarne Junction " Q " run. B—Will not apply when 10.0 a.m. from China Clay Co.'s Siding to Boscarne Junction and 1.45 p.m. Wenford to Wadebridge " O " trains run.

15. One of the many charming features of the branch was the stream-fed water tank in Pencarrow Wood. Designed for the early diminutive locomotives, it is clear that the filler pipe (known as the bag) was inclined upwards. The angle was even greater with the ex-GWR engines. The date is 25th March 1960. (J.J.Smith)

16. The goods for Wenford approaches Dunmere Wharf on the same day. The guard was required to stand on the A389 with a red flag in hand and the driver was ordered to "whistle freely". (J.J.Smith)

17. No. 30587 is returning from Wenford on 17th August 1959 and is passing Dunmere Wharf. It had originally been known as "Borough Bounds Wharf" and ceased to handle local traffic on 14th May 1969. (P.Hay)

18. No. 30585 has stopped on its journey to Wenford on 10th July 1961 to deposit some wagons in the siding at Dunmere. Its train stands behind the camera while the guard clips the points. (R.C.Riley)

19. No. 08377 brings a loaded train from Wenford over the A389 at Dunmere on 28th September 1978. The van is on the site of the siding which had once handled grain for a nearby mill. The rails were still to be seen in the roadway nearly 20 years later. (D.Mitchell)

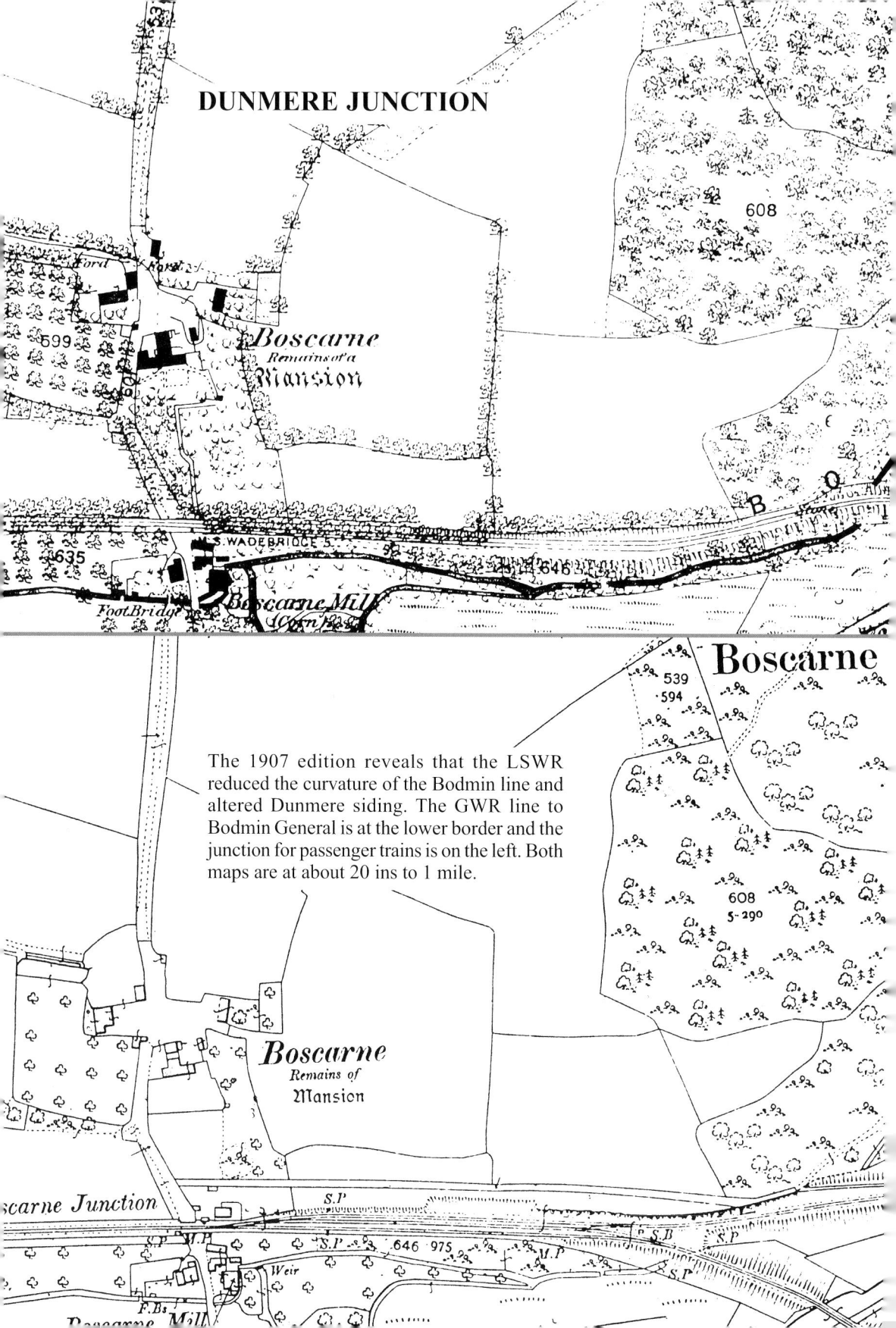

The 1907 edition reveals that the LSWR reduced the curvature of the Bodmin line and altered Dunmere siding. The GWR line to Bodmin General is at the lower border and the junction for passenger trains is on the left. Both maps are at about 20 ins to 1 mile.

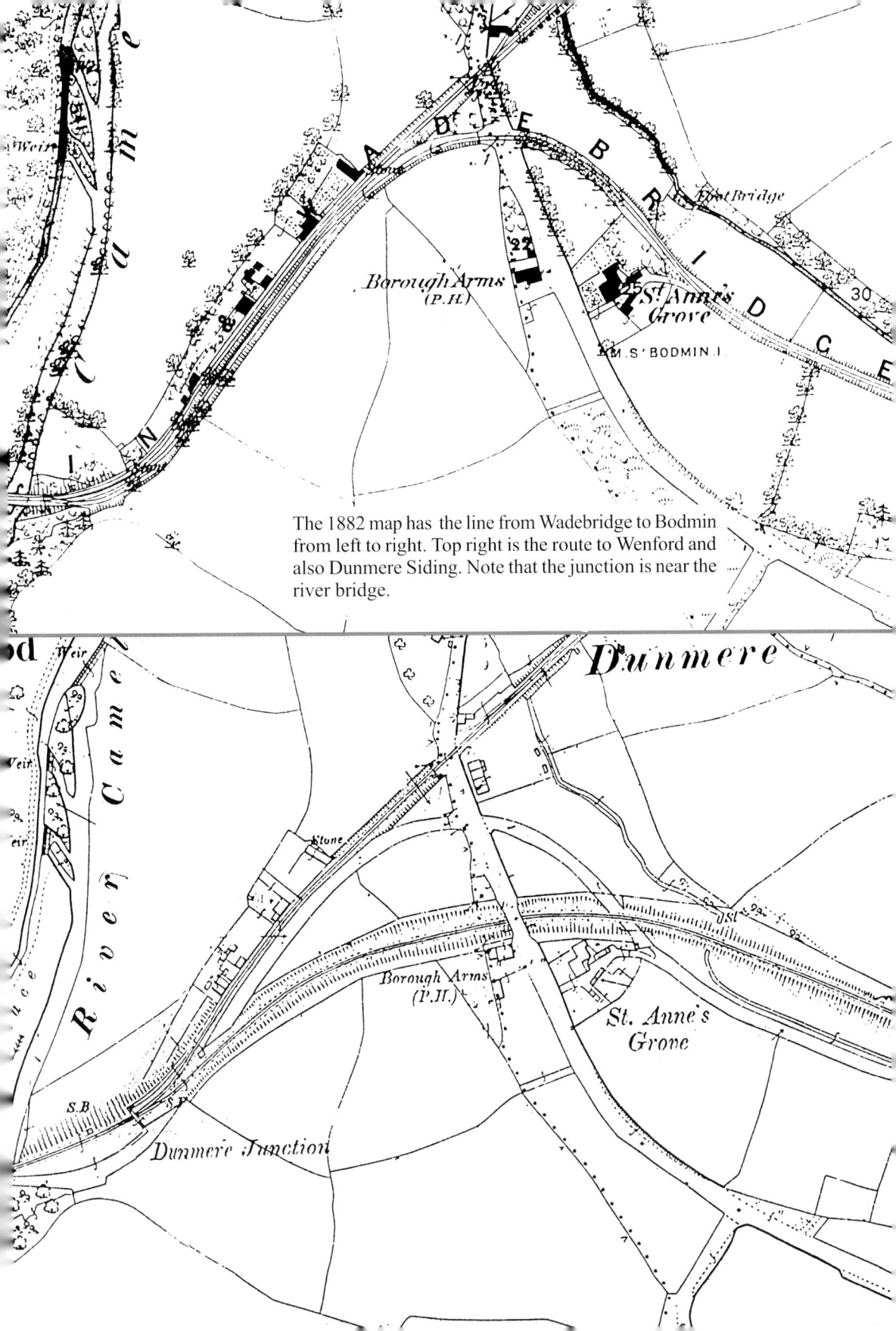

The 1882 map has the line from Wadebridge to Bodmin from left to right. Top right is the route to Wenford and also Dunmere Siding. Note that the junction is near the river bridge.

20. No. 30585 approaches the gate which isolated the branch which was worked as a "one engine in steam" siding. Seen on the right on 19th August 1954 is the line to Bodmin North. (R.M.Casserley)

21. The same viewpoint on 6th October 1982 features no. 08945, the permanent way trolley hut and the ex-LSWR trackbed, which had been last used by trains on 30th January 1967. (D.Mitchell)

22. Looking in the opposite direction to the two previous pictures, we witness no. 30586 leaving the Padstow-Bodmin North line on 17th May 1962, bound for Wenford. In the background is the ground frame and bridge over the River Camel. A footbridge once spanned the line near the smoking guards van. (S.C.Nash)

23. Dunmere Junction box was unlocked by the guard. He then set the points and signals to allow his train onto the branch; he relocked the frame, walked to Boscarne Junction box with the single line tablet and then walked back to his train. The box had been on the opposite side of the track until 1914. (R.C.Riley)

BOSCARNE JUNCTION

24. Boscarne Junction box (left) is at the west end of four parallel tracks. Class 4500 2-6-2T no. 4585 is working the 3.28pm Wadebridge to Bodmin Road on 19th August 1954 and is on the WR reversible line. Next is the exchange siding and beside it is the SR reversible line. The Well Tanks in this and the next picture are on the Wenford Goods line. (R.M.Casserley)

25. No. 30587 has arrived with assorted wagons from Wenford on 2nd March 1956. The signal is of the LSWR lattice type and controlled trains coming from Bodmin North. (J.J.Smith)

26. Following dieselisation of passenger services in the area in 1964, a shuttle service between Bodmin North and a new low level "platform" was instituted on 15th June. The AC railbuses were fitted with folding steps. No. W 79977 has its lowered at 4.30pm on 24th July 1964. (J.H.Aston)

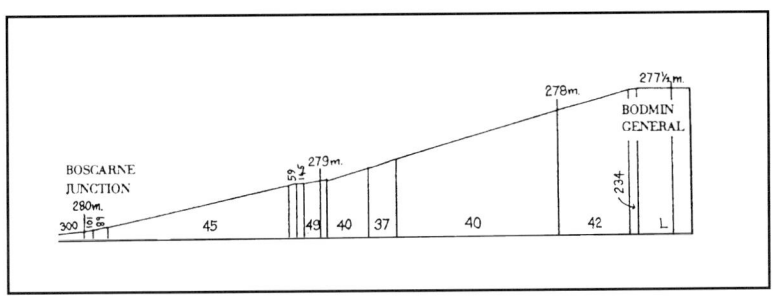

27. Passengers changing to a conventional DMU on the Padstow-Bodmin Road service had to walk past the oil lights and climb onto a new timber-built platform. These "exchange platforms" were accessible only by rail. (S.C.Nash)

July 1924

LOSTWITHIEL and FOWEY—(Road Motor Service).
Week Days only.

	mrn	mrn	mrn	mrn	aft	aft	aft	aft	aft	aft		
Lostwithiel........dep.	7 10	8 20	9 5	1015	1 0	2 30	4 10	5 10	6 10	7 0	..	..
Torfrey Cross Roads(for	7 35	8 45	9 30	1040	1 25	2 55	4 35	5 35	6 35	7 25	..	..
Fowey.....(Golant) arr.	7 50	9 0	9 45	1055	1 40	3 10	4 50	5 50	6 50	7 40	..	..
	mrn	mrn	mrn	mrn	aft	aft	aft	aft	aft	aft		
Fowey....(Golant) dep.	7 5	8 15	9 5	1140	1 20	3 15	4 20	4 55	6 5	7 40	..	..
Torfrey Cross Roads(for	7 20	8 30	9 20	1155	1 35	2 30	4 35	5 10	6 20	7 55	..	..
Lostwithiel 26, 31 arr.	7 45	8 55	9 45	1220	2 0	3 55	5 0	5 35	6 45	8 20	..	..
Rail Tickets available. Heavy luggage not conveyed.

28. A differently styled railbus was recorded at 3.09pm on 13th June 1966. The converging lines in the foreground were for freight traffic only, the points being worked from the ground frame on the right. The platforms went out of use briefly from 16th April 1966, as two Bodmin Road-Padstow trains per day reversed here (twice) to run via Bodmin North. This was a temporary arrangement before reversion to the earlier timetable prior to cessation of passenger services in January 1967. (Lens of Sutton)

November 1941

Miles		a.m		a.m	a.m	a.m	a.m		**Week Days only** p.m	p.m	p.m	p.m		p.m E	p.m S	p.m		p.m E	p.m S	p.m		p.m	
	Lostwithiel......... dep	7 10	..	8 5	9 0	1015	1140	..	1235	1 30	2 25	3 55	..	4 45	4 55	6 5	..	7 0	7 10	8 10	..	9 35	..
3¾	Golant...............	7 19	..	8 14	9 9	1024	1149	..	1244	1 39	2 34	4 4	..	4 54	5 4	6 14	..	7 9	7 19	8 19	..	9 44	..
5¼	Fowey.............. arr	7 25	..	8 20	9 15	1030	1155	..	1250	1 45	2 40	4 10	..	5 0	5 10	6 20	..	7 15	7 25	8 25	..	9 50	..

Miles		a.m		a.m	a.m	a.m	non S		**Week Days only** p.m S	p.m	p.m		p.m		p.m		p.m		p.m		p.m	p.m	
	Fowey .... dep	7 30	..	8 30	9 30	1115	12 0	..	1255	1 50	3 35	..	4 20	..	5 35	..	6 25	..	7 35	..	9 5	10 5	..
1½	Golant...............	7 36	..	8 36	9 36	1121	12 6	..	1 1	1 56	3 41	..	4 26	..	5 41	..	6 31	..	7 41	..	9 11	1011	..
5¼	Lostwithiel..... arr	7 45	..	8 45	9 45	1130	1215	..	1 10	2 5	3 50	..	4 35	..	5 50	..	6 40	..	7 50	..	9 20	1020	..

E Except Saturdays   S Saturdays only

29. No. 08945 stands near the level crossing gates on 6th October 1982, having just arrived with loaded wagons from Wenford. No. 37274 is about to be coupled up for the journey to Fowey. The signal box seen in picture 24 had closed on 17th December 1967, when the line on the right was truncated at its east end to form a siding. (D.Mitchell)

30. The route from Bodmin General and the track on the left of the previous picture remained dormant from 1983 to 1996. A new platform is seen under construction on the site of the former SR running line on 4th June 1996. (T.E.Corin)

31. The platform and loop were completed in time for the official opening, seen here on 14th August 1996. Public service commenced the next day. The DMU vehicles are nos 53980 and 52054. (M.Dart)

32. This is almost the same camera angle as used in picture 28, but 31 years later. The gap in the trees accommodated the Camel Trail instead of the line to Wenford. No. 62 *Ugly* was built by Robert Stephenson Hawthorn in 1950. There were a maximum of four weekday trains to this station in the Summer of 1997. (M.Turvey)

SOUTH OF BOSCARNE JUNCTION

33. Two photographs from 5th May 1964 illustrate the high cost of heavy mineral transport in hilly terrain. Two class Ns were required on the steep gradient to Bodmin General. No. 31849 has just passed over the road to Nantstallon and is climbing at 1 in 45. (S.C.Nash)

34. At the rear of the train is no. 31840, giving the guard's ear drums a substantial flexing. The labour involved in sheeting so many wagons can be imagined. St. Lawrence Hospital Platform was in this vicinity from 1906 to 1917. (S.C.Nash)

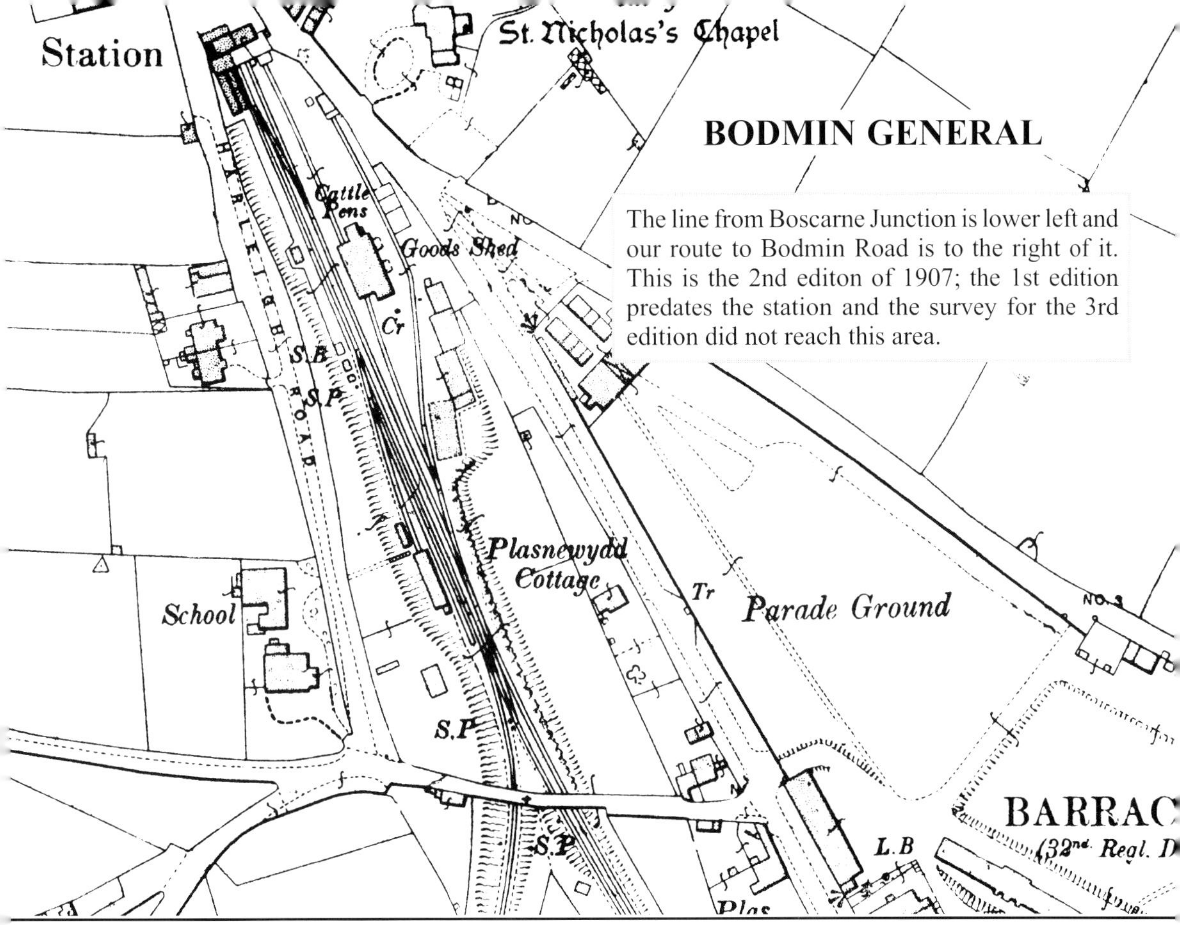
Station
St. Nicholas's Chapel
BODMIN GENERAL
Cattle Pens
Goods Shed
HARLEIGH ROAD
S.B
S.P
Cr
Plasnewydd Cottage
School
Tr
Parade Ground
S.P
S.P
L.B
BARRAC
(32nd. Regl. D

The line from Boscarne Junction is lower left and our route to Bodmin Road is to the right of it. This is the 2nd editon of 1907; the 1st edition predates the station and the survey for the 3rd edition did not reach this area.

35. Although further from the town centre than the SR terminus, the station had the advantage of a spacious uncongested approach and of being close to the gates to the barracks (left). Military traffic was a good source of revenue. (M.Dart coll.)

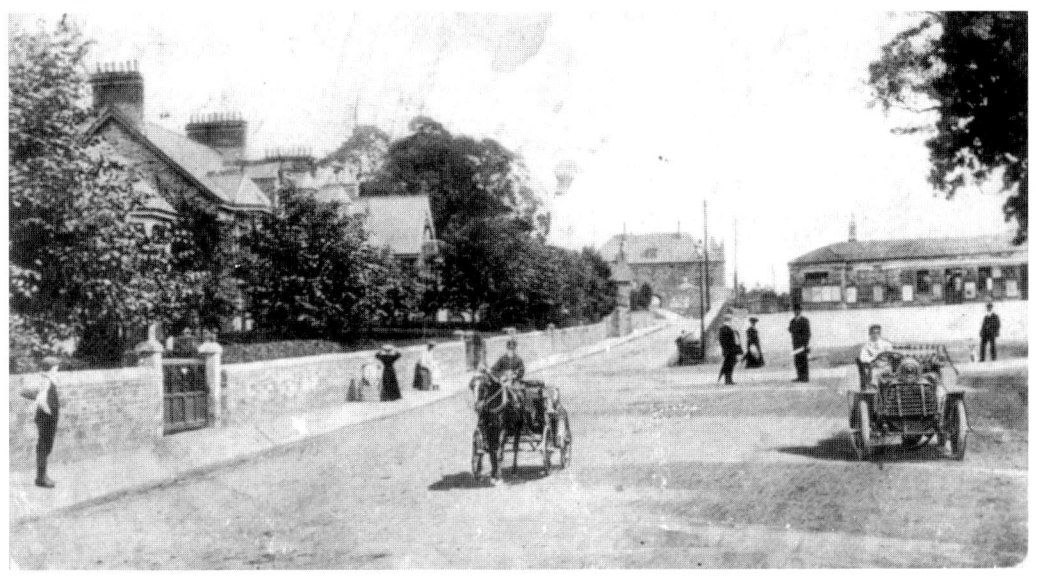

36. A down train from Bodmin Road arrives behind 2-6-2T no. 4552 on 23rd May 1935. The line on the right curves round the south of the town to Boscarne Junction. (H.C.Casserley)

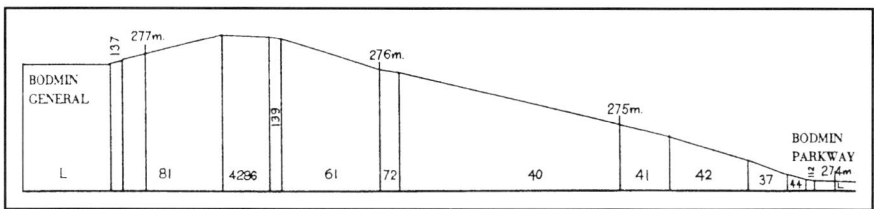

37. The station was decorated imaginatively in 1948. Agricultural produce, fertiliser and equipment still formed a substantial part of railway revenue at that time. For example, 505 trucks of livestock were handled in 1936, the peak year for that traffic in that decade. (M.Dart coll.)

38. A view from the platform end on 22nd June 1956 includes an ex-LSWR class O2 0-4-4T no. 30200 running round the train that would form the 6.30pm to Wadebridge. On the shed road is class 4500 2-6-2T no. 4526. Locomotives ceased to be shedded here after April 1962. (M.Dart)

39. A panorama from the bridge seen in picture 36 includes the locomotive shed and water tower (left), a train departing for Bodmin Road and also the goods shed. In 1935, 31408 parcels generated £1535 but 31523 produced only £641 in 1937. (H.Cowan)

40. Another photograph from September 1956 gives us a closer look at the goods yard. To the right of the crane is a demountable wagon body. No. 4526 is one of the highly successful 4500 class of which 13 survive. Public goods facilities were withdrawn on 1st May 1967. (H.Cowan)

41. A train from Bodmin Road has just arrived and the locomotive leaves its coaches while passengers walk towards them. It appears that two more are being attached before departure for Wadebridge. On the left is a demountable van body or container. These were used in the battle against the road hauliers. (Lens of Sutton)

July 1948

Miles		a.m		a.m	a.m	a.m	a.m		p.m	p.m	p.m	p.m		p.m	p.m	p.m		p.m	p.m	p.m		p.m
							S							E	S			E	S			
	Lostwithiel......dep	7 10	..	8 5	9 0	1015	1140	..	1235	1 30	2 25	3 55	..	4 45	4 55	6 5	..	7 0	7 10	8 10	..	9 35
3¾	Golant...............	7 19	..	8 14	9 9	1024	1149	..	1244	1 39	2 34	4 4	..	4 54	5 4	6 14	..	7 9	7 19	8 19	..	9 44
5¼	Fowey...........arr	7 25	..	8 20	9 15	1030	1155	..	1250	1 45	2 40	4 10	..	5 0	5 10	6 20	..	7 15	7 25	8 25	..	9 50

Miles		a.m		a.m	a.m	a.m	non		p.m	p.m	p.m		p.m		p.m		p.m		p.m		p.m	p.m
									S													
	Fowey..........dep	7 30	..	8 30	9 30	1115	12 0	..	1255	1 50	3 35	..	4 20	..	5 35	..	6 25	..	7 35	..	9 5	10 5
1½	Golant...............	7 36	..	8 36	9 36	1121	12 6	..	1 1	1 56	3 41	..	4 26	..	5 41	..	6 31	..	7 41	..	9 11	1011
5¼	Lostwithiel.......arr	7 45	..	8 45	9 45	1130	1215	..	1 10	2 5	3 50	..	4 35	..	5 50	..	6 40	..	7 50	..	9 20	1020

E Except Saturdays   S Saturdays only

September 1963

Mls.		am			am			am			am			pm			pm			pm			pm		pm
—	Lostwithiel .. dep	7 5	..	..	8 5	..	..	9 5	..	..	1015	..	..	1225	..	..	2 30	..	..	4 40	..	5 55	..	6 55
3¾	Golant Halt	7 14	..	..	8 14	..	..	9 14	..	..	1024	..	..	1234	..	..	2 39	..	..	4 49	..	6 4	..	7 4
5¼	Fowey .. arr	7 20	..	..	8 20	..	..	9 20	..	..	1030	..	..	1240	..	..	2 45	..	..	4 55	..	6 10	..	7 10

Mls.		am			am			am		am			pm			pm		pm			pm		pm
—	Fowey .. dep	7 30	..	..	8 25	..	..	9 25	..	1045	..	..	2 5	..	..	4 20	..	5 17	..	..	6 15	..	7 15
1¾	Golant Halt	7 35	..	..	8 30	..	..	9 30	..	1050	..	..	2 10	..	..	4 25	..	5 22	..	..	6 20	..	7 20
5¼	Lostwithiel .. arr	7 45	..	..	8 40	..	..	9 40	..	11 0	..	..	2 20	..	..	4 35	..	5 32	..	..	6 30	..	7 30

42. The station closed to passengers on 30th January 1967 but was still in good order when photographed in October 1972, when it was only used for the reversal of clay trains. The signal box closed on 17th December 1967 and the South West Group of the Great Western Society took a lease on the engine shed in 1969. (C.L.Caddy)

43. On their open day in July 1970, the society gave rides on *Camel*, a platelayers trolley that had spent most of its life in the shed seen in pictures 20 and 21. (F.Dumbleton)

44. GWS members sit beside their coach as a BR class 08 diesel leaves for Bodmin Road on 22nd August 1971. Despite a preservation presence, the signal box and locomotive shed were demolished. The water tower was removed to Didcot Railway Centre. (M.Dart coll.)

45. The open day on 22nd July 1972 saw the GWS's class 1361 ex-GWR 0-6-0ST no. 1363 and Hawksworth coach no. 7372 working short trips. The society vacated the site in 1976. (M.Dart coll.)

46. Two photographs from 28th September 1978 show sheeted wagons and the method of operation of clay trains. No. 08377 arrives from Boscarne Junction and runs into the relatively short loop which restricted the length of trains. (D.Mitchell)

47. The guard rides back on the steps of the locomotive, having altered the points by hand. The brake van will be removed and placed at the other end of the train before proceeding to Bodmin Road, where the procedure will be repeated. (D.Mitchell)

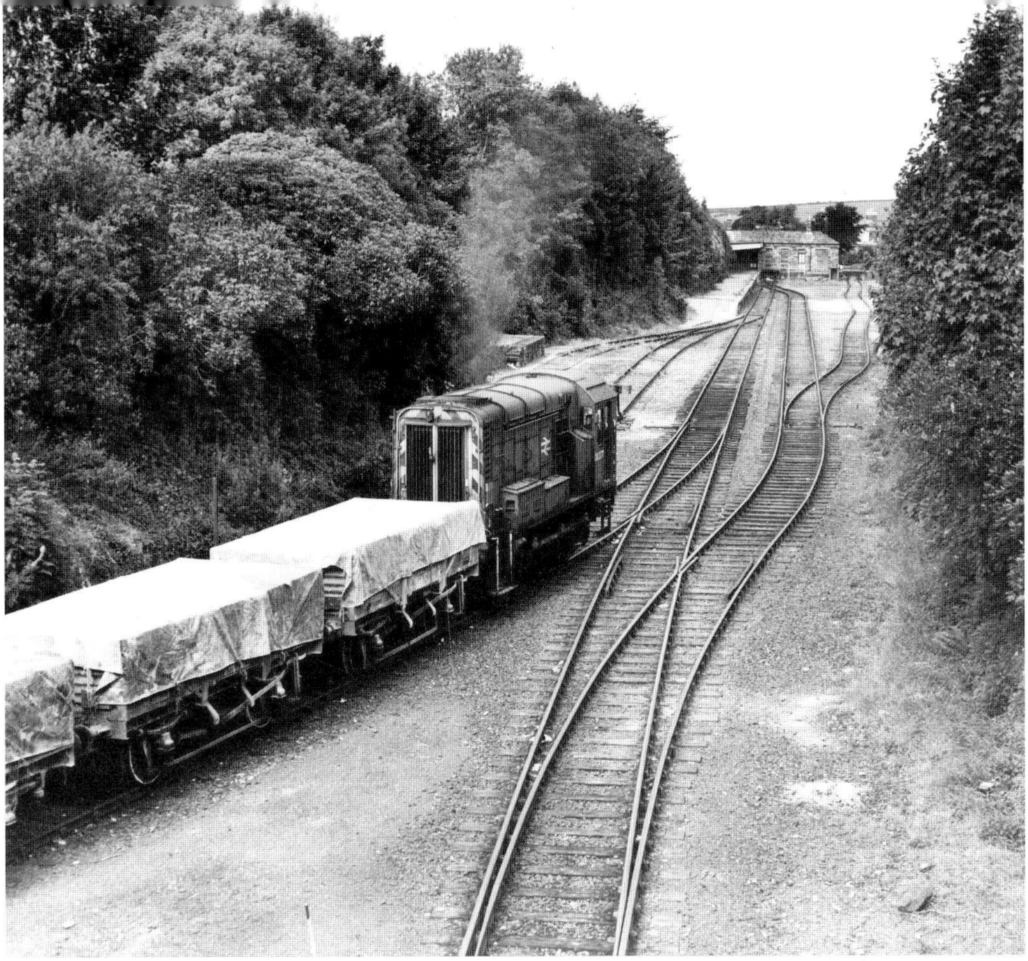

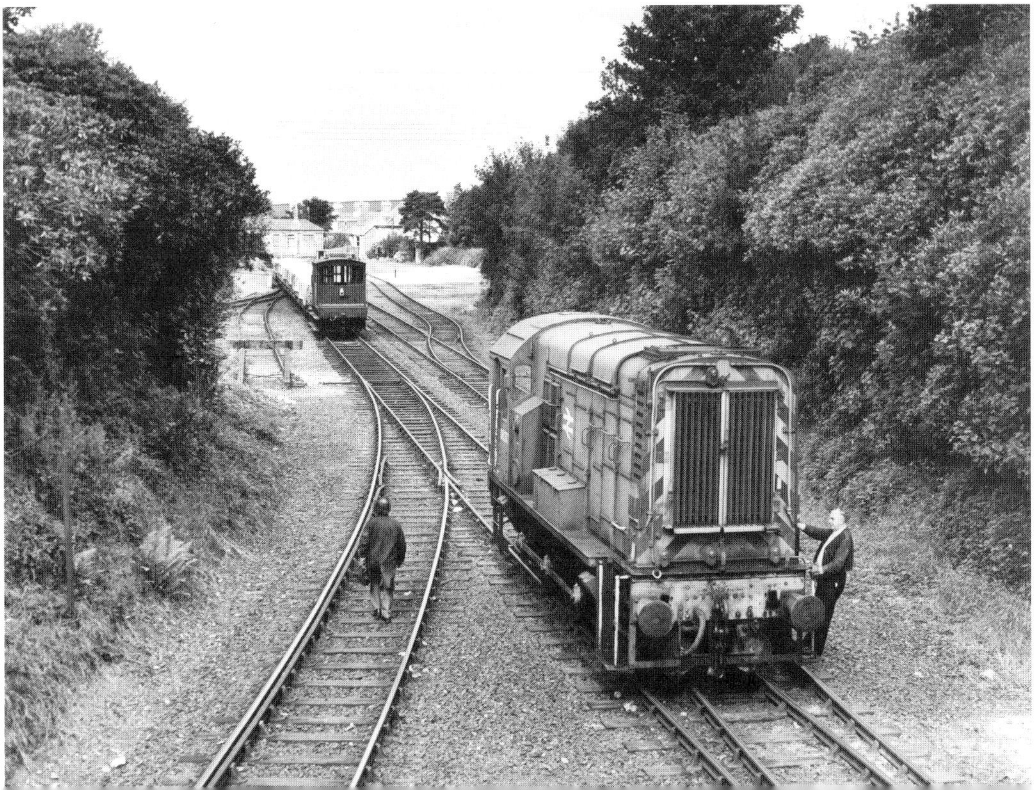

48. The BWR made remarkable progress on the site and recommenced a service to Bodmin Road on 17th June 1990. Hunslet 0-6-0ST *Swiftsure* is ready to depart, while ex-GWR no. 7752 stands in the siding. It was on the line from March until September 1994 and was photographed on 3rd May. (T.Heavyside)

49. An extensive workshop building was erected in 1987 to facilitate locomotive restoration work. This is a view from the buffer stops in March 1996 with part of the fleet of 22 coaches standing in the platform and two of the four DMU vehicles in the loop. (V.Mitchell)

50. A view from the Boscarne Junction line includes the ground frame for the junction and the curious and complex provision for pedestrians to pass over the lines and under the road which is on a dangerously narrow bridge. (V.Mitchell)

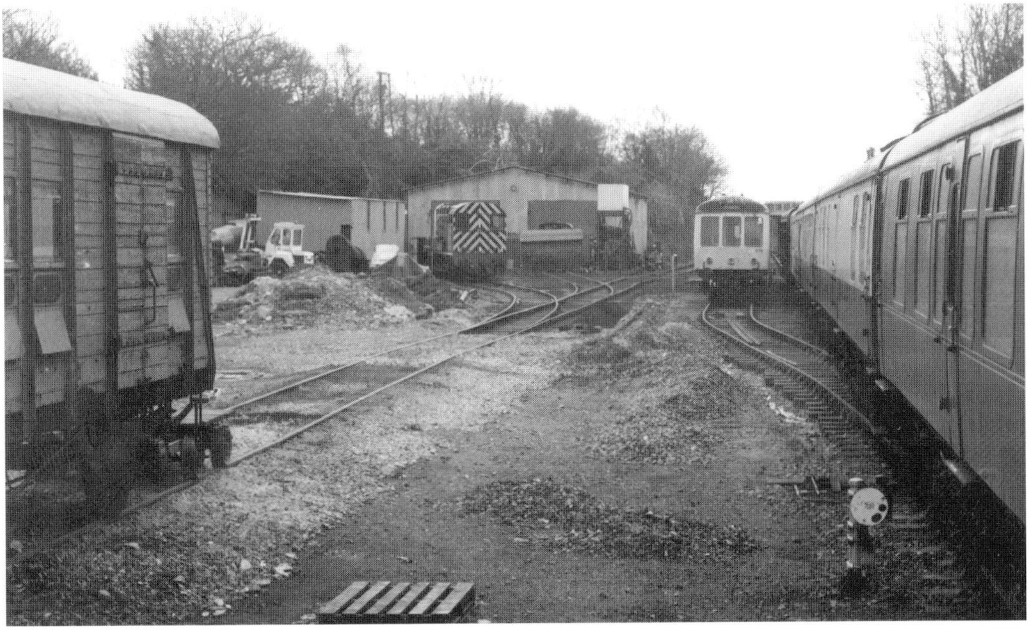

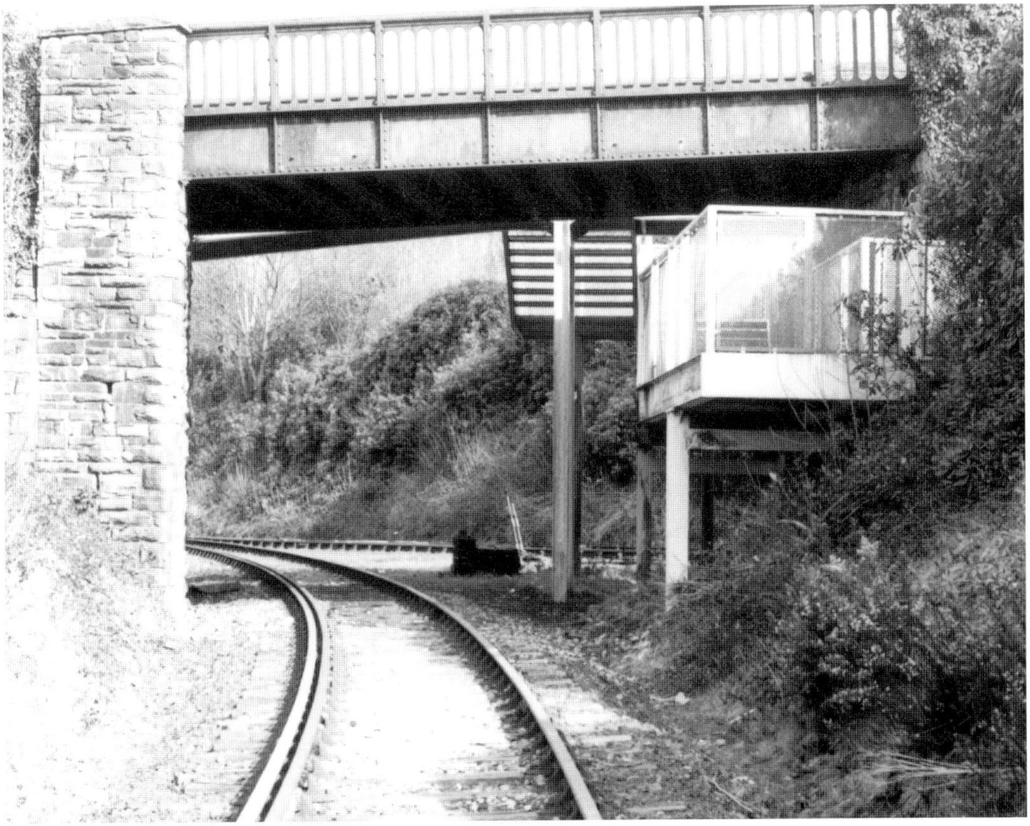

SOUTH OF BODMIN GENERAL

51. Approaching the station on 29th April 1983 is no. 37207 with Chipman's weedkilling train on its last visit. In the left background is Walker Lines Industrial Estate where a siding had been provided in 1973 for Fulford Trumps. It was used for a few years for agricultural equipment. (T.Heavyside)

52. The Walker Lines siding was reopened by Fitzgerald Lighting on 2nd December 1989 and was in use until 27th July 1991, a BWR class 20 diesel locomotive usually moving wagons to and from Bodmin Road. Traffic recommenced (Mondays only) on 20th September 1996, this diminutive 60hp Fowler *Progress* of 1940 being used to shunt the VGA wagons back into the siding. No. 50042 *Triumph* was in store in October 1997. (V.Mitchell)

53. Coleslogett Halt, two miles from Bodmin General, was opened on 17th April 1992 to serve Bodmin Farm Park. Subsequently it was used by passengers travelling to Cardinham Woods. *Swiftsure* shelters in the shade of the trees on its way to Bodmin Parkway on 4th June 1996. (T.E.Corin)

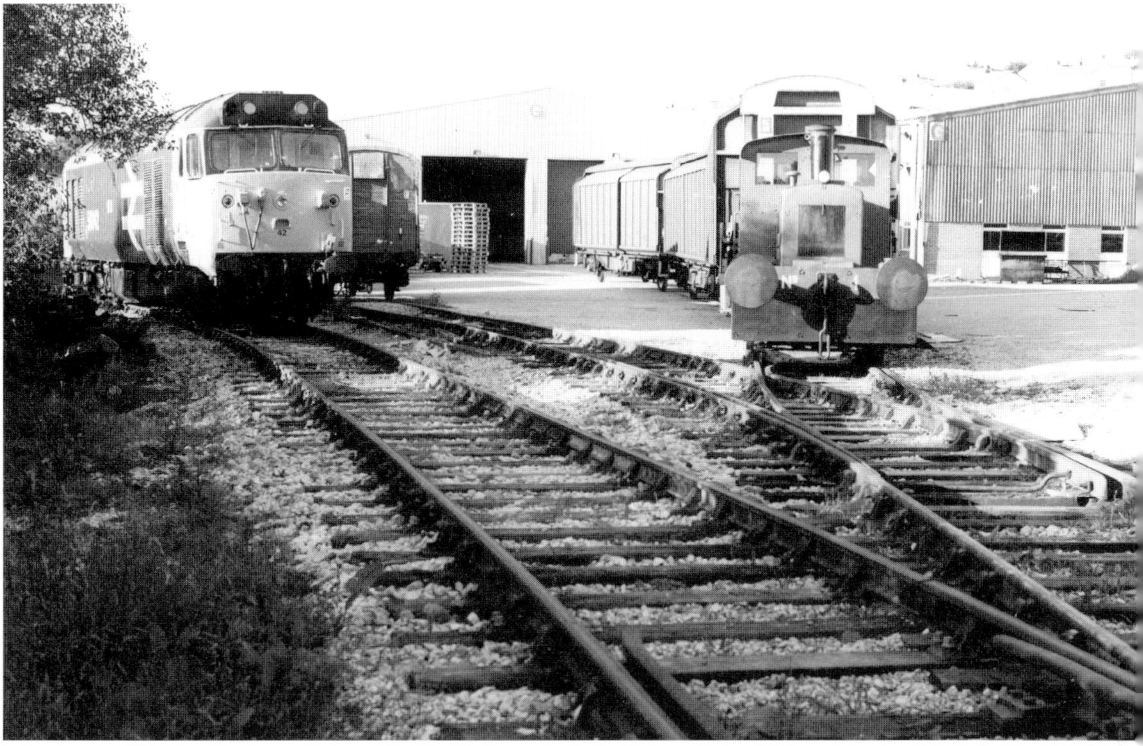

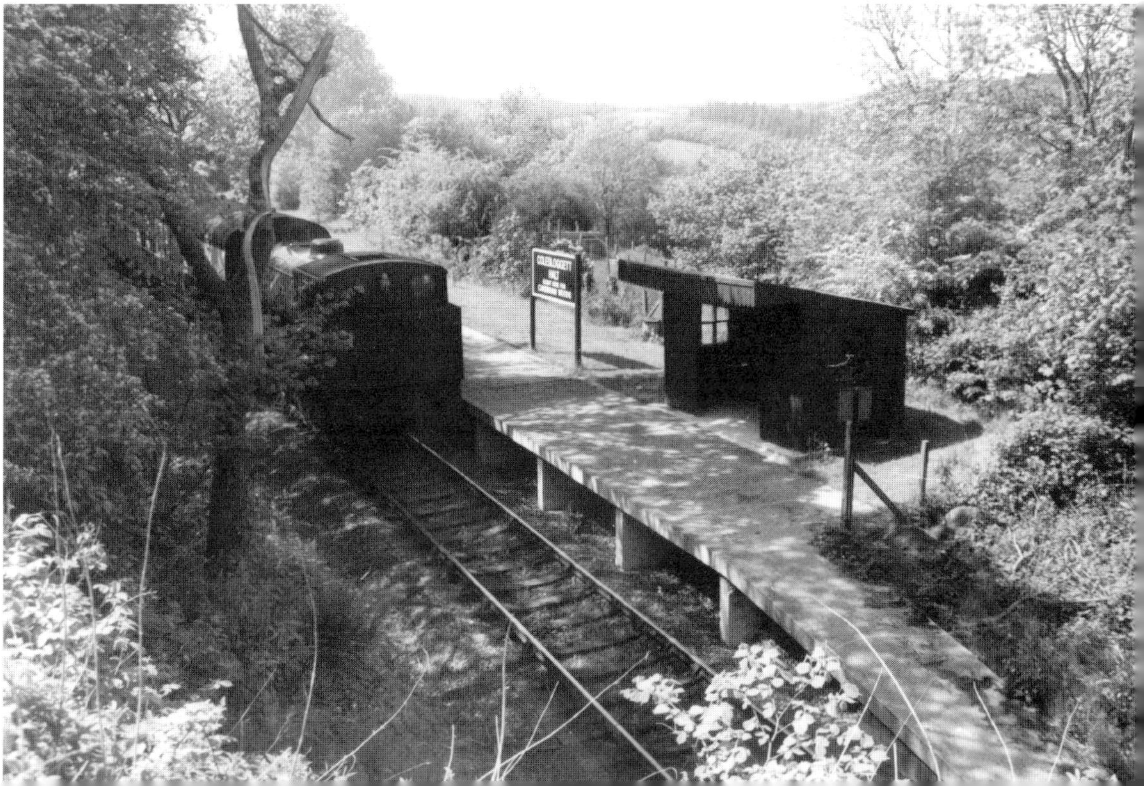

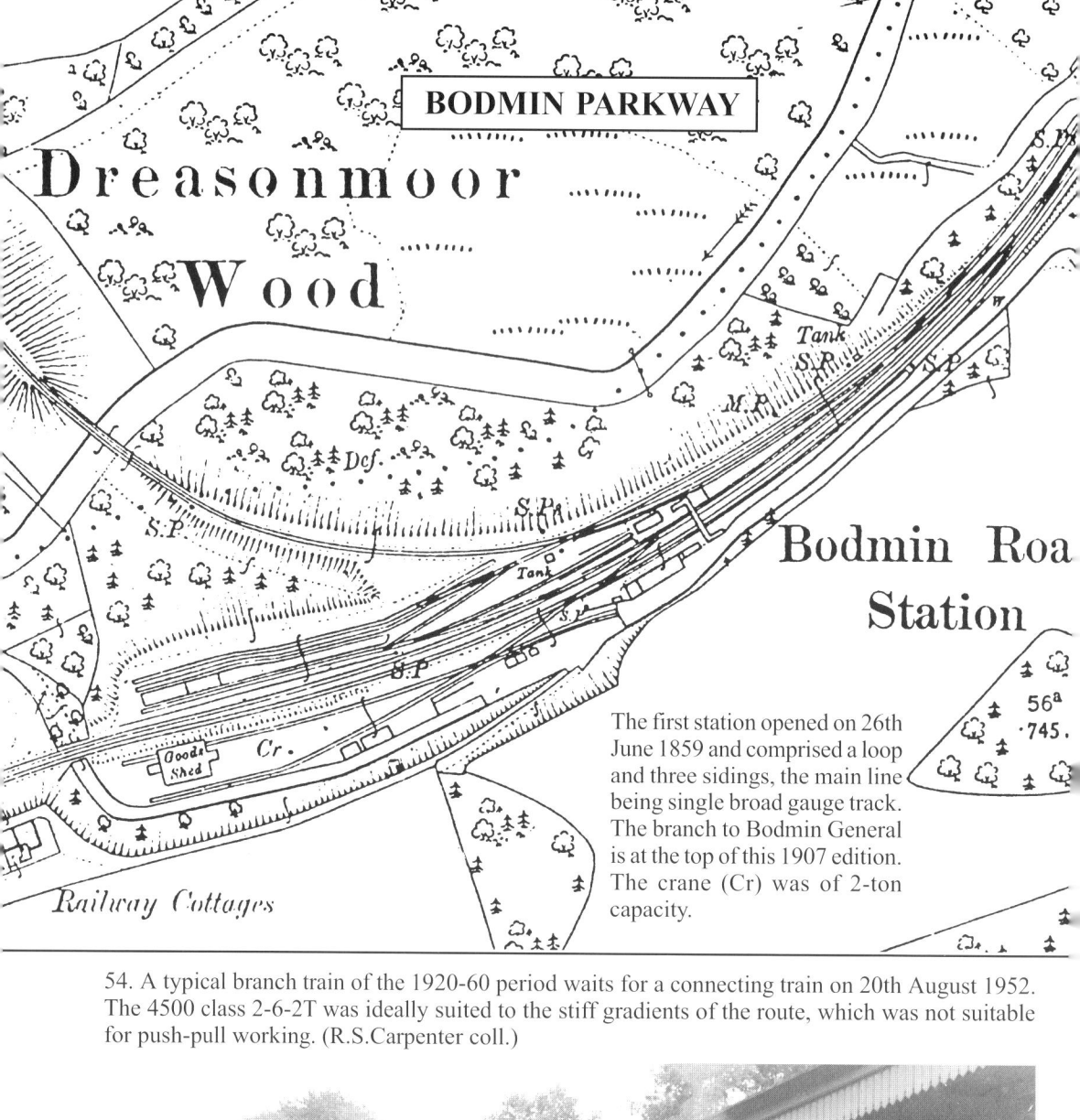

BODMIN PARKWAY

Dreasonmoor Wood

Bodmin Road Station

Railway Cottages

The first station opened on 26th June 1859 and comprised a loop and three sidings, the main line being single broad gauge track. The branch to Bodmin General is at the top of this 1907 edition. The crane (Cr) was of 2-ton capacity.

54. A typical branch train of the 1920-60 period waits for a connecting train on 20th August 1952. The 4500 class 2-6-2T was ideally suited to the stiff gradients of the route, which was not suitable for push-pull working. (R.S.Carpenter coll.)

55. The unusual water crane was photographed on 19th August 1954 while 2-6-2T no.4584 was being refreshed. There were two connections to the up main line in use between 1915 and 1963. (H.C.Casserley)

56. Recorded on the same day is class 4300 2-6-0 no.6300 presenting a good clean exhaust while working a westbound freight. The branch driver gives a friendly wave. (R.M.Casserley)

57. Returning holidaymakers gather on the up platform on 17th August 1958, as a down train waits to depart. Also included is the goods shed and the brazier which was used to prevent the water valve freezing. The original shed had been to the right of the main line. (A.E.Bennett)

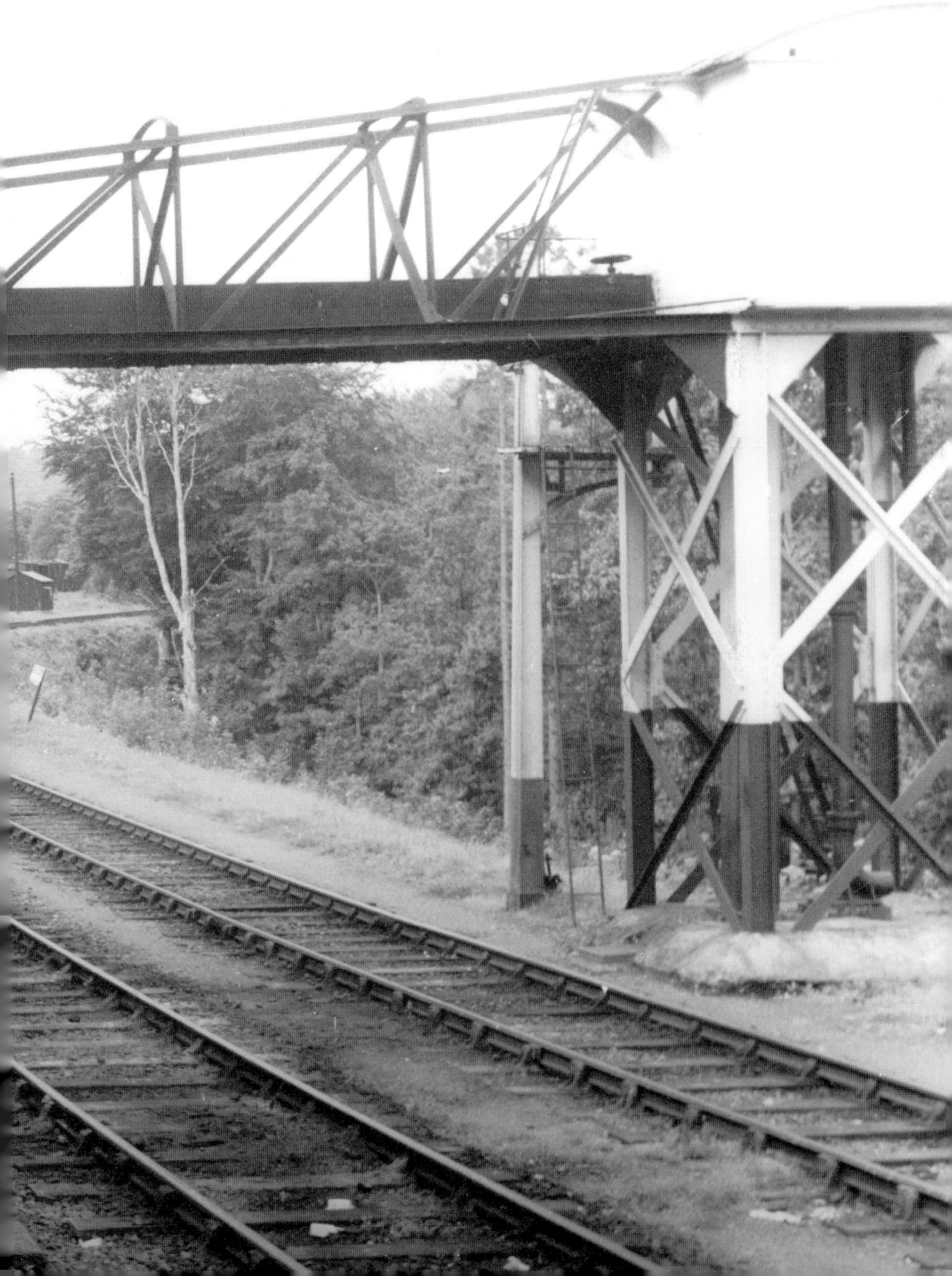

58. Although undated, this photograph can be placed between 1964 and 1967. The DMU era on the branch resulted in much less work for the signalman. The line curves to Bodmin General on the right. (Lens of Sutton)

59. The sidings seen in the background of the previous picture are seen more closely on 12th September 1973, with nos D4008 and D4007 in attendance. A goods exchange platform was in use here between 1887 and 1892. This was used as a cattle dock in later years. (D.Mitchell)

60. The goods shed road and the branch platform line were both taken out of use on 27th March 1968, goods facilities having been withdrawn on 4th November 1963. However, an extension of the former track served ECLP china clay works until December 1966. No.46015 was captured on film on 17th June 1977. (T.Heavyside)

Other views of this station and the route so far can be found in our *Branch Lines around Bodmin*.

61. Pictured the same day was the same locomotive rising on the 1 in 65 gradient with empty "clay hoods". The uninsulated telegraph and telephone wires were soon to be consigned to history. (T.Heavyside)

62. A photograph from 29th April 1983 reveals that the up platform had been lengthened to accommodate eight coaches. No.50048 is working a Plymouth-Penzance service. The name was changed from Bodmin Road to Bodmin Parkway on 4th November 1983. (T.Heavyside)

63. We now have two views from March 1995. This shows that only the footbridge and signalbox remained from the GWR era; the latter was in use as a buffet and had ceased its original function on 30th November 1983 but was reopened occasionally for special movements. New buildings were erected on both platforms in 1989. (V.Mitchell)

64. At the west end of the up platform is the connection to the BWR, the main line of which is on the right. Ruston & Hornsby diesel no.3 *Lec* stands with stock awaiting restoration. (V.Mitchell)

WEST OF
BODMIN PARKWAY

65. The west portal of the 88-yd long Brownqueen Tunnel was photographed from a train ascending the 1 in 71 gradient behind two diesels on 21st August 1961. This section of the main line was doubled in 1893. (M.Dart)

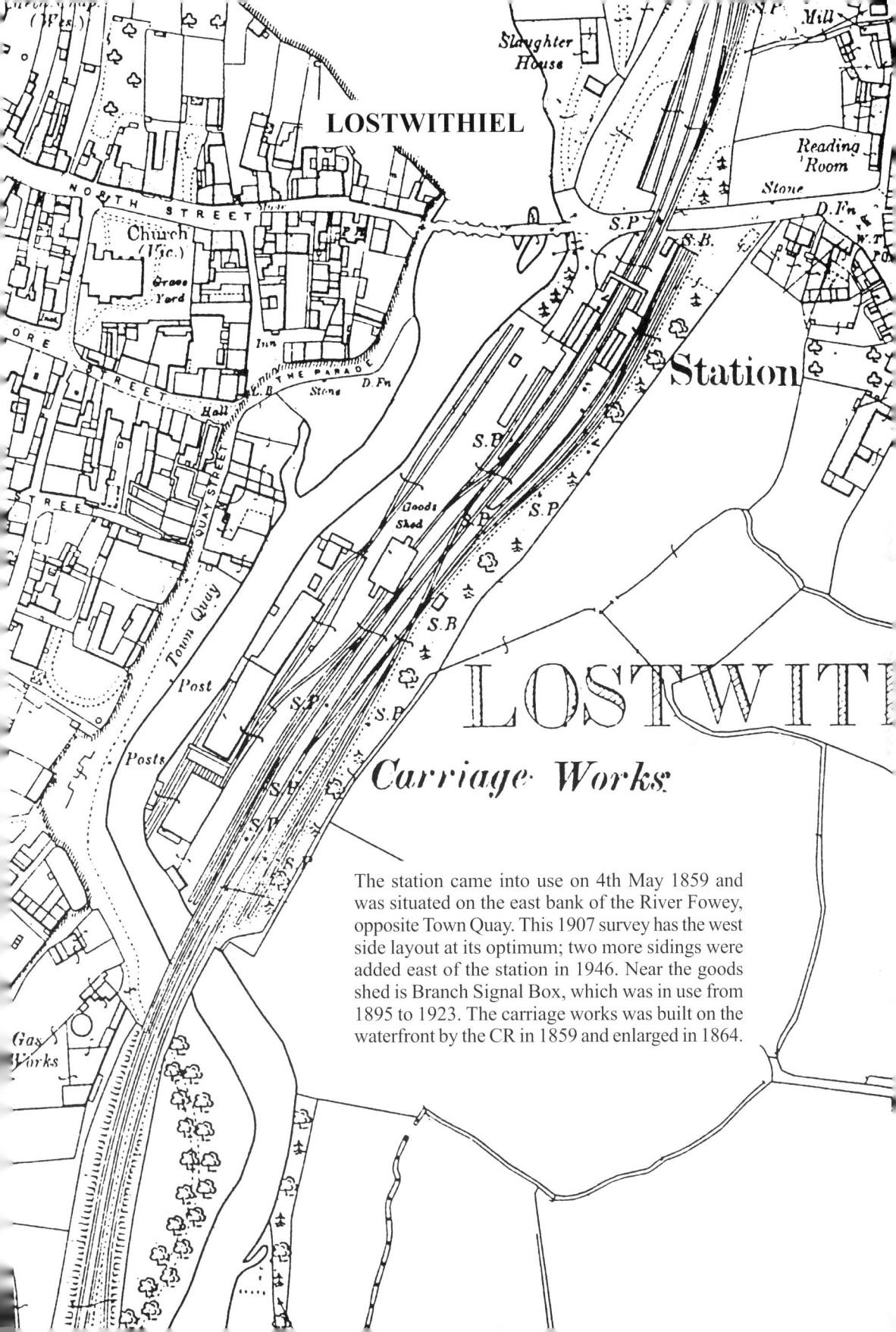

The station came into use on 4th May 1859 and was situated on the east bank of the River Fowey, opposite Town Quay. This 1907 survey has the west side layout at its optimum; two more sidings were added east of the station in 1946. Near the goods shed is Branch Signal Box, which was in use from 1895 to 1923. The carriage works was built on the waterfront by the CR in 1859 and enlarged in 1864.

66. A postcard view towards the level crossing includes a clerestorey coach in the Fowey branch train formation. Unlike Bodmin Road, the footbridge was not totally enclosed. The bay platform was in use from 1895 and the main line to Par was doubled in 1896. (Lens of Sutton)

67. Lighting was perfect for this study of a driver oiling up, a fireman recuperating and an autocoach in GWR livery. Note the folding steps for use at halts with ground level platforms. (M.Dart Coll)

68. The panorama from the footbridge on 18th August 1954 includes 2-6-0 no.6309 westbound and the 1893 signal box. This had a 63-lever frame but only 39 were in use in 1997. The gates were replaced by full lifting barriers on 1st June 1969. (H.C.Casserley)

69. A siding was provided east of the station for the Unigate Milk Depot in 1932. Six-wheeled milk tankers are in evidence as no.5915 *Trentham Hall* departs with a Penzance - Plymouth train on 10th July 1955. (R.C.Riley)

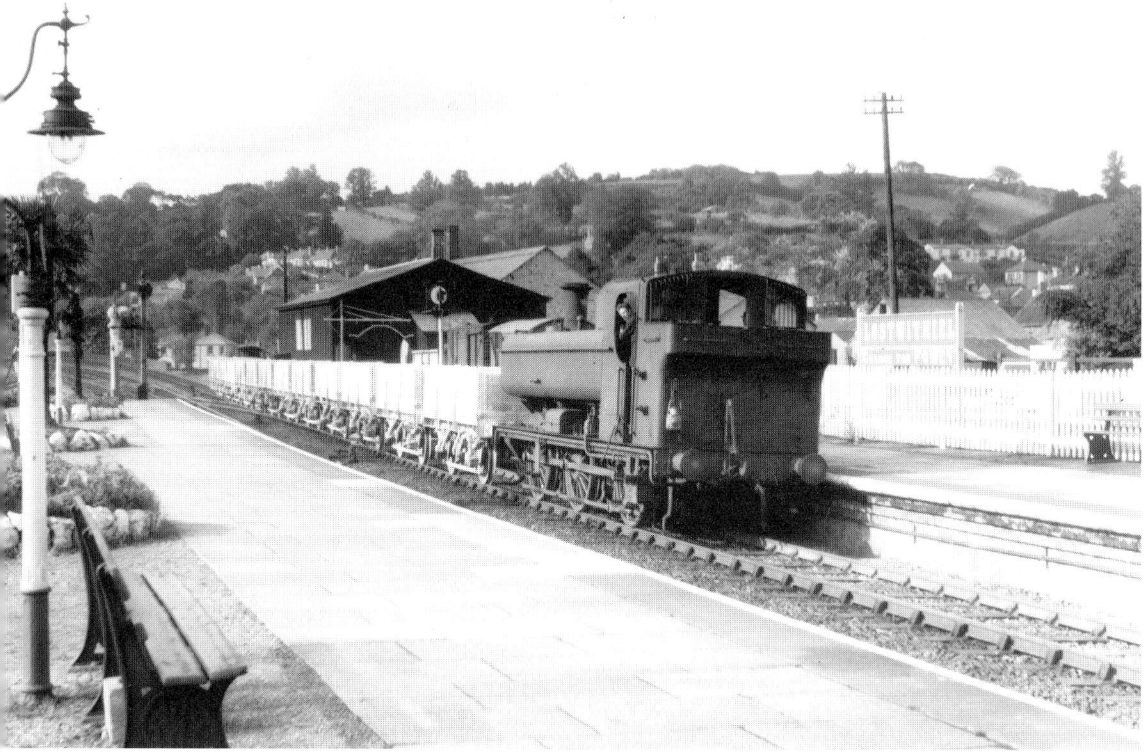

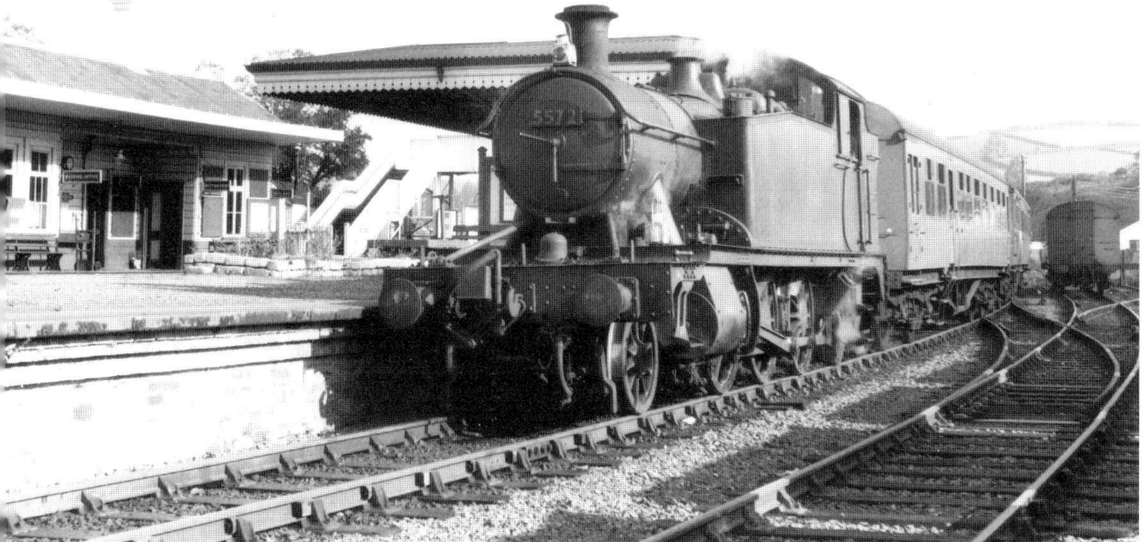

70. The end of the train is still in the goods yard as no.9655 shunts on 23rd September 1960. Beyond the goods shed is the former carriage workshop. (R.C.Riley)

71. Photographed on the same day on the Fowey service was class 4575 no.5572, one of a select few fitted for push-pull working in the valleys of South Wales and displaced by dieselisation in that area. The locomotive later went to Didcot for preservation. (R.C.Riley)

72. No.25216 runs into the down loop with "clay hoods" from the St.Austell area. The locomotive in the siding will be attached at the far end and will then haul the train down the branch to Fowey. (T.Heavyside)

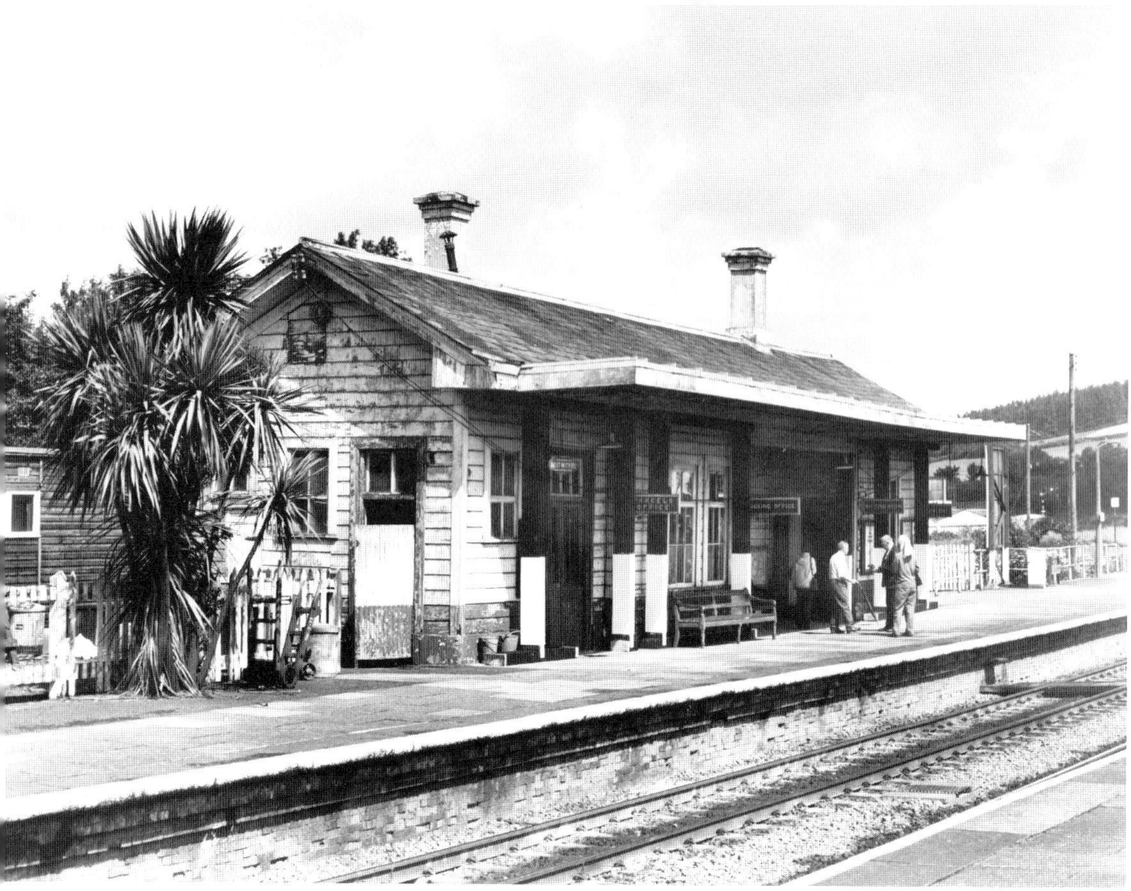

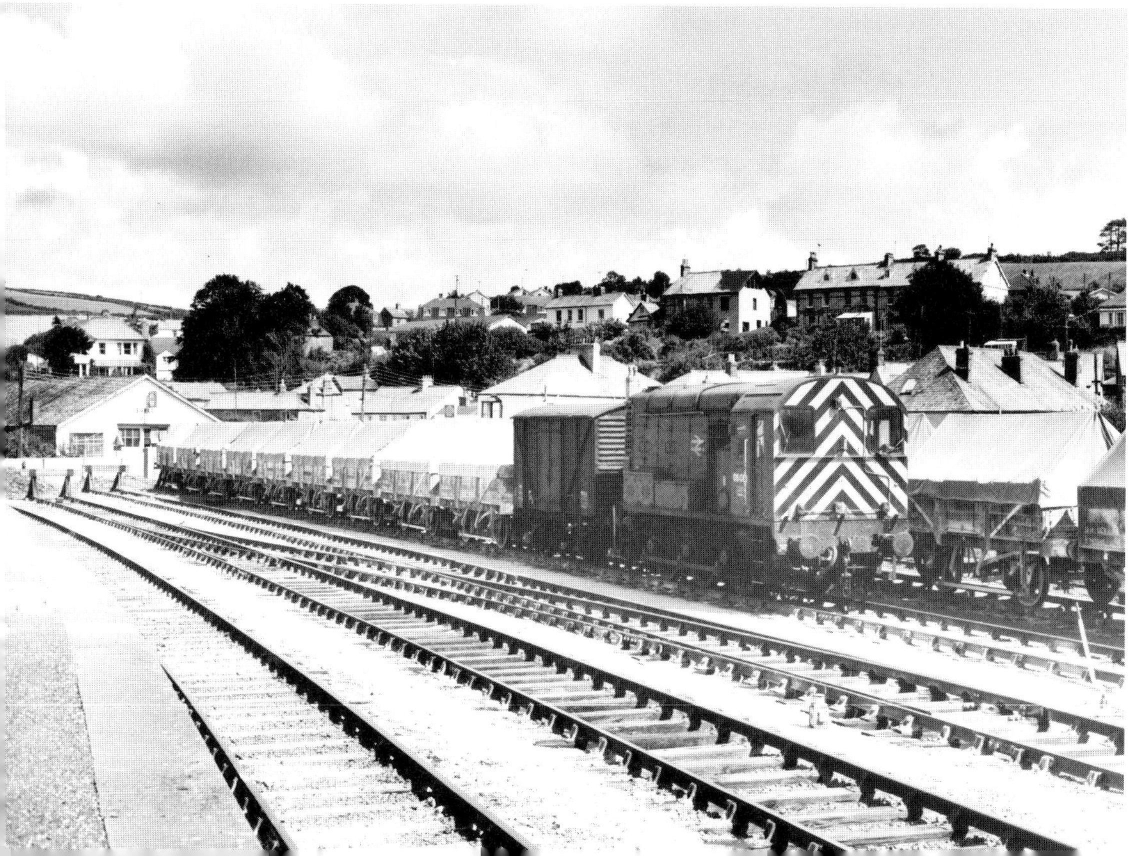

73. The historic station building was in poor condition by 1978 and required temporary props. Optimists listed it a Grade II structure but it was later deemed beyond salvation and was dismantled in 1981 for reconstruction at St.Agnes. This never happened and the material was destroyed. The down side building was re-erected at Marsh Mills on the Plym Valley Railway. (D.Mitchell)

74. No.08091 leaves its train from Wenford in the down sidings on 16th August 1978. The "clay hoods" were of 12- ton capacity; their successors held nearly three times as much. (D.Mitchell)

75. A train of empties comes off the branch on 30th March 1984, while a loaded train arrives on the up main line. On the left are two of the former carriage works buildings. (P.G.Barnes)

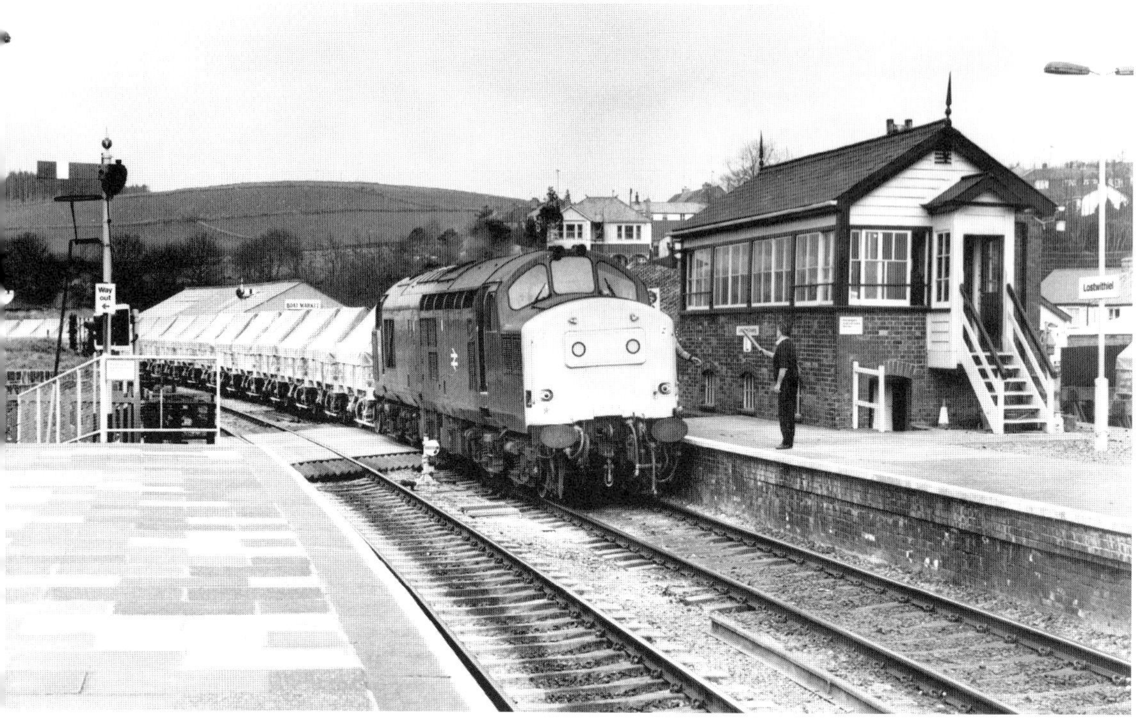
Way out
Lostwithiel

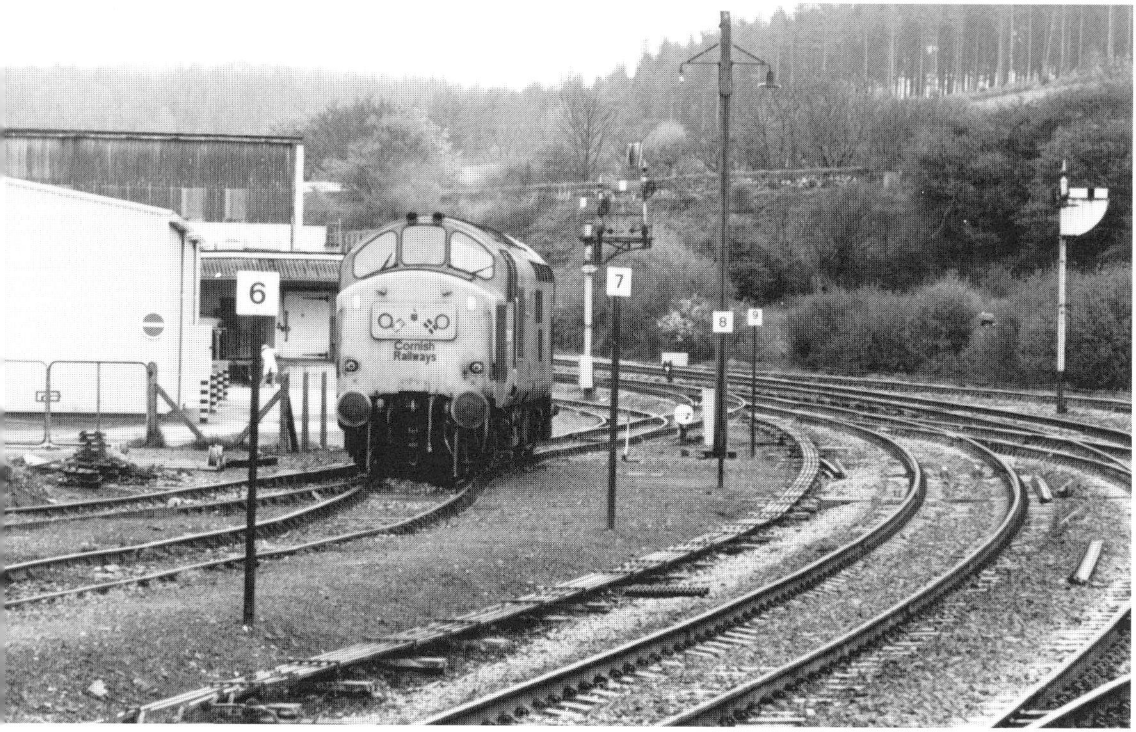
6
7
8
9
Cornish Railways

76. Having run round its loaded train in the down loop on 10th April 1984, no.37176 runs over the level crossing again as the driver collects the token for the Fowey branch. (D.Mitchell)

77. Bearing a short-lived freight operating name, no.37207 takes refuge in one of the up sidings on 1st May 1987. The left signal arm is for the up loop and the figures indicate the stopping positions for up passenger trains. (P.G.Barnes)

78. There now follow three pictures from 3rd October 1997. First, the ancient and modern signal box. While some levers are missing, others are out of use and painted white. Four operated point motors. A panel at the far end controlled the Bodmin Parkway area. (V.Mitchell)

79. The independent third line over the River Fowey for the branch was removed in November 1972 and so we arrive with an empty clay train on the down line. Two class 47 RES locomotives run light to Plymouth, having left their mail trains at St.Blazey for servicing. (V.Mitchell)

80. Having run around its train in the down loop, no.37671 returned to the bay to collect a misdirected wagon, seen also in the previous picture. The new building was officially opened by the mayor on 18th November 1982, but was unstaffed when photographed. (V.Mitchell)

SOUTH OF LOSTWITHIEL

81. An early colour postcard producer chose the northern end of the branch as a subject. The River Fowey is also included. The line to Par is in the background of this and the next two pictures. (M.Dart coll)

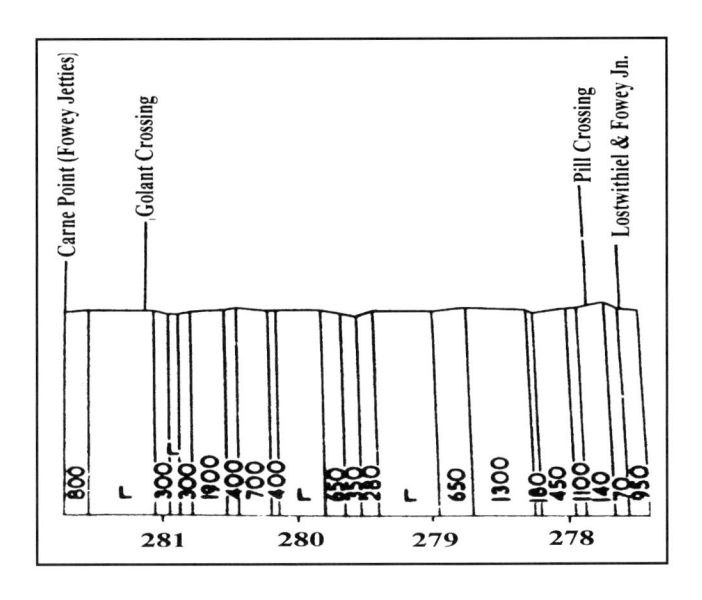

82. This cab view was taken shortly before picture 79. The ground signal was used to call the driver into the down platform. Extensive semaphore systems were difficult to find east of this location by that time. (V.Mitchell)

83. Class 50 no.50015 was aptly hauling 50 wagons when photographed on 1st May 1987 starting its journey down the valley. Note that the distant signal is apparently much further from the junction than in picture 81, as the junction had been moved west. (P.G.Barnes)

GOLANT HALT

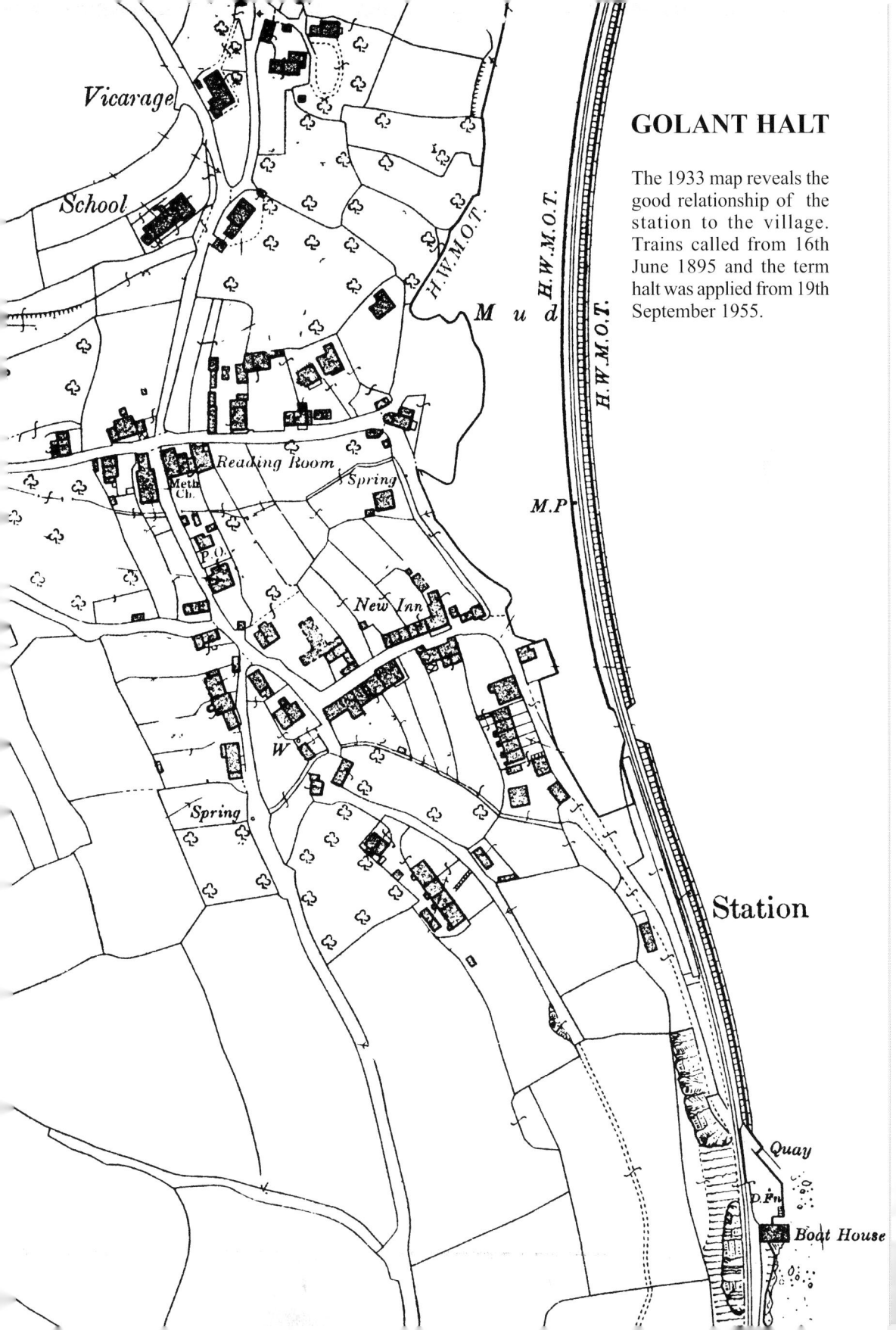

The 1933 map reveals the good relationship of the station to the village. Trains called from 16th June 1895 and the term halt was applied from 19th September 1955.

84. The construction of the railway in 1869 created a sheltered tidal lagoon. A five-coach train stands at the single platform. The peaceful valley has been used for period film settings. A few shots have been ruined by the sudden appearance of a clay train. (M.Dart coll.)

85. No roads traverse the valley and so the halt was of great value to villagers. This is the 14.35 from Lostwithiel on 7th September 1964. These units began working on the branch in April 1961. A two-car DMU appeared on an evening mystery tour from Par via Lostwithiel on 29th July 1964 and also on the last day, 2nd January 1965. (A.Muckley)

Closed	Reopened
2nd April 1917	1st November 1917
1st January 1940	9th February 1942
24th August 1942	3rd October 1942
2nd May 1944	2nd October 1944

86. A view from the cab of an up train in 1997 includes the unprotected crossing on the little used road to the quay. The platform began at the point where the rails pass out of view. (V.Mitchell)

87. A gull creates a reflection in the still water as no.37142 disturbs the peace on 28th September 1978. At least it is transitory, unlike the equivalent number of lorries. (D.Mitchell)

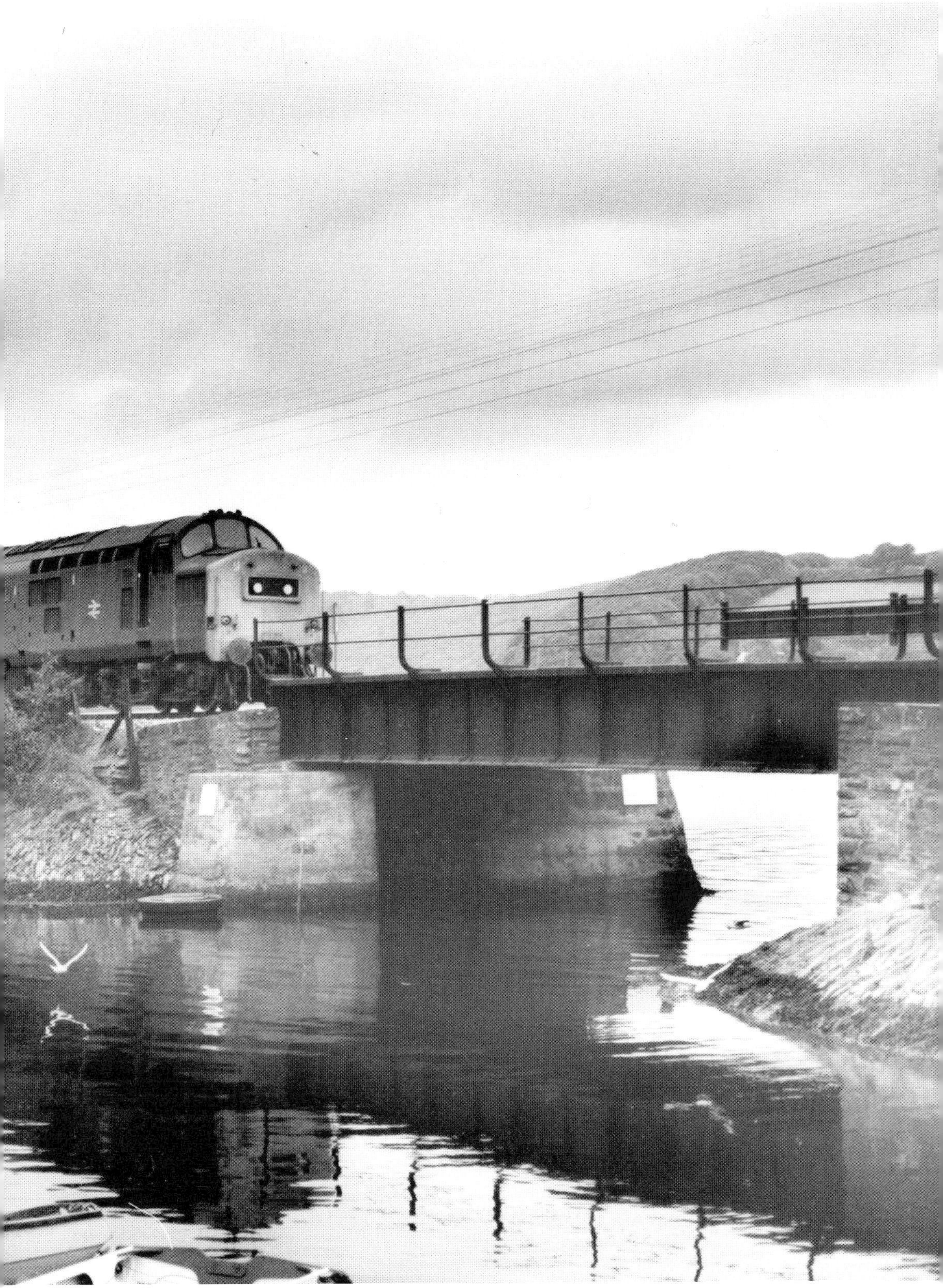

FOWEY JETTIES

The first edition of 1882 has the GWR's 1869 branch from Lostwithiel at the top and the CMR's 1874 system below, the two being separated by Carne Point. The 1876 Fowey station is lower left.

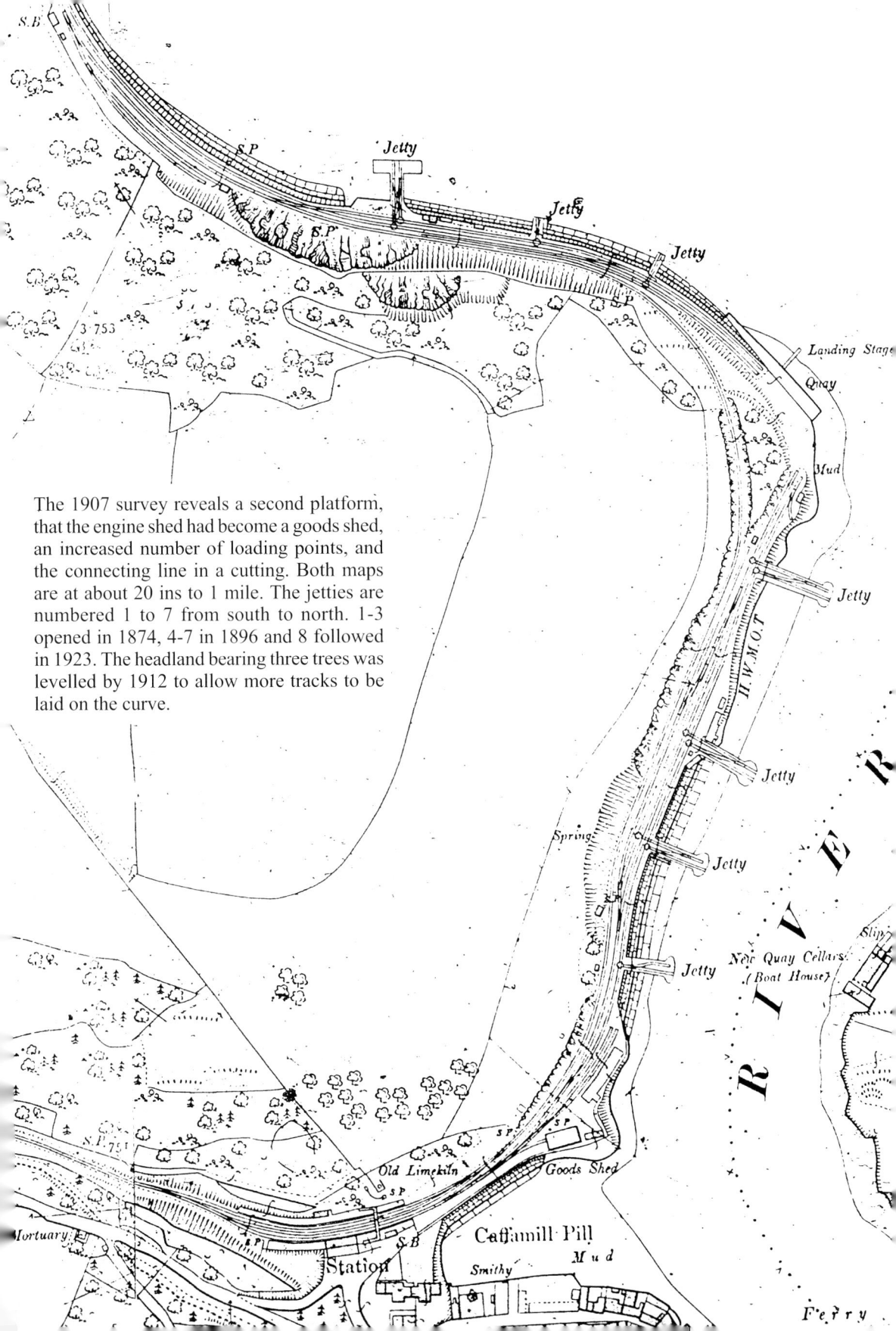

The 1907 survey reveals a second platform, that the engine shed had become a goods shed, an increased number of loading points, and the connecting line in a cutting. Both maps are at about 20 ins to 1 mile. The jetties are numbered 1 to 7 from south to north. 1-3 opened in 1874, 4-7 in 1896 and 8 followed in 1923. The headland bearing three trees was levelled by 1912 to allow more tracks to be laid on the curve.

88. The original jetties are featured in this southward view from the sail era. It is evident that there was not a standard way of loading wagons with casks. The wagons were shunted to and from the turntables by horses. (M.Dart coll.)

90. No.8 jetty is included in this photograph of Carne Point sidings and 0-4-2T no.1419, taken on 2nd September 1954. The single autocoach is bound for Lostwithiel. (R.C.Riley)

89. The steamship era brought larger vessels and improved material handling systems, such as the conveyor in the background. This eastward panorama has the running line on the left and features nos 3 and 4 jetties. (M.Dart coll.)

91. A closer look at no.8 jetty on the same day shows that it had two lines. Both were parallel to the vessel unlike nos 1 to 6. No.7 had turntables at the end of the usual two tracks from the shore, these also being on a single line alongside the ship. (R.C.Riley)

92. On the non-mechanised jetties, transhipment continued to be very labour intensive, the changeover from casks to bags making little difference. While bagged clay was often conveyed in vans to avoid sheeting, this method precluded its unloading by crane. (ECC)

93. The entire route to Par together with all the jetties and sidings at Fowey were sold to English China Clays on 1st July 1968. The company retained and eventually relaid only those lines north of no.8 jetty, thus no.37187 was recorded at the BR boundary on 19th November 1983. Later that day, the BR-organised tour became the last locomotive hauled train at Boscarne Junction. Also included is ECC-owned class 10 no.D3497 (derelict) and the weighbridge shed. (D.Mitchell)

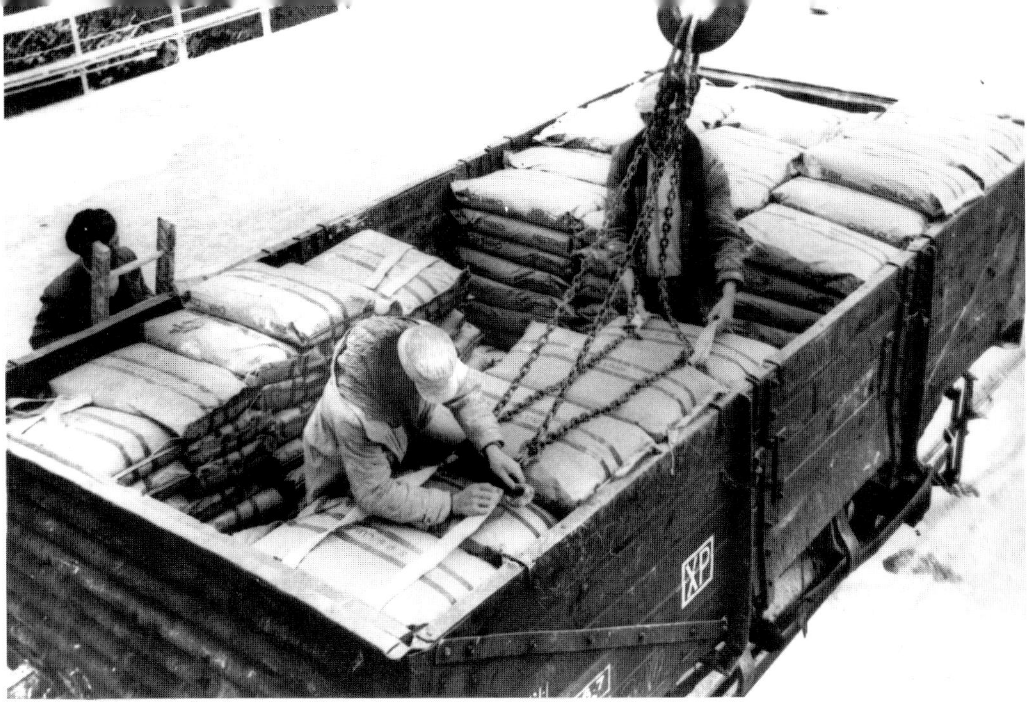

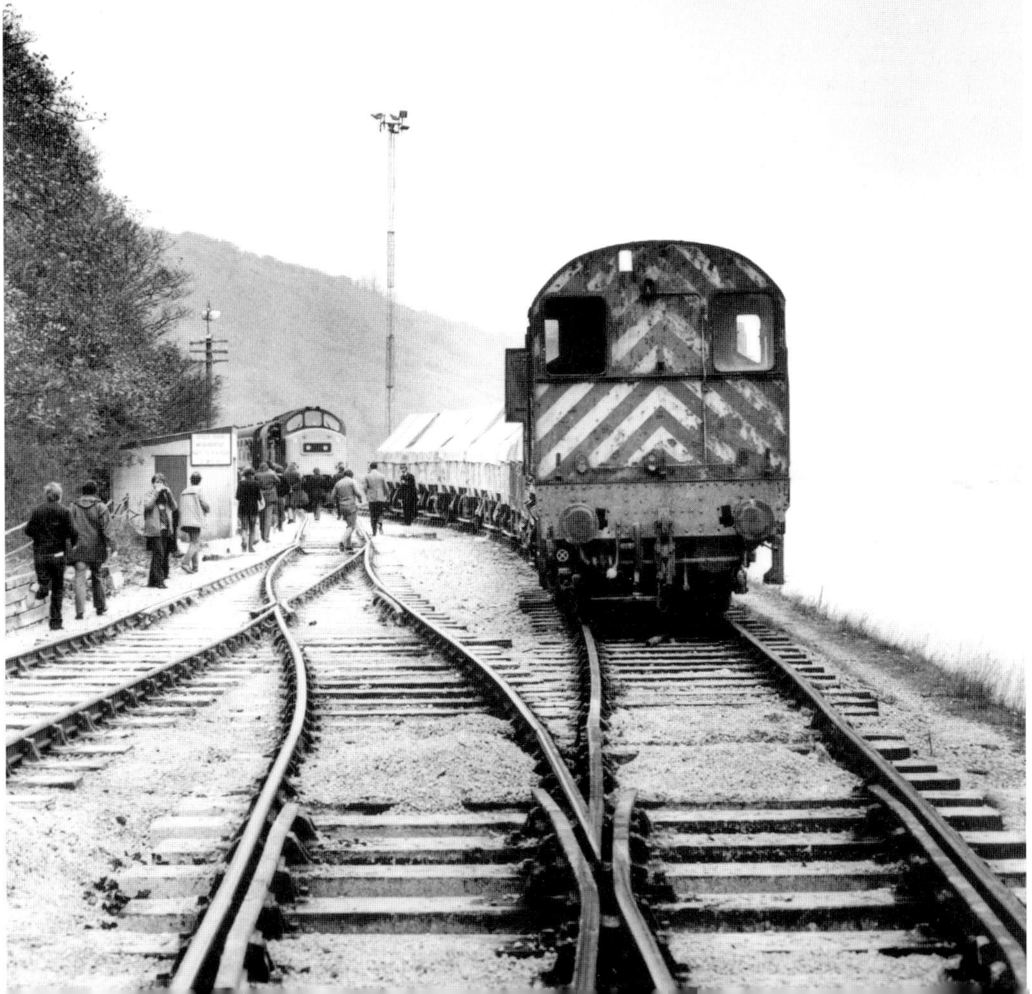

94. Looking in the other direction on the same day, we see the no. 8 jetty again with the *MV Dinonna* being loaded. Carne Point signal box had stood on our viewpoint from 20th March 1925 until 23rd August 1954. Its two predecessors had been on the other side of the tracks. (D.Mitchell)

95. A view north through the discharge shed in 1987 shows a "clay hood" being emptied and another departing empty, having been moved across the site on a traverser. The wagon is in the fully lifted position. (P.G.Barnes)

96. Once over the discharge pit, the end door was released and the opposite end of the wagon hoisted up. Underground conveyor belts transported the clay to one of several storage bins from which the ships were loaded. (ECC)

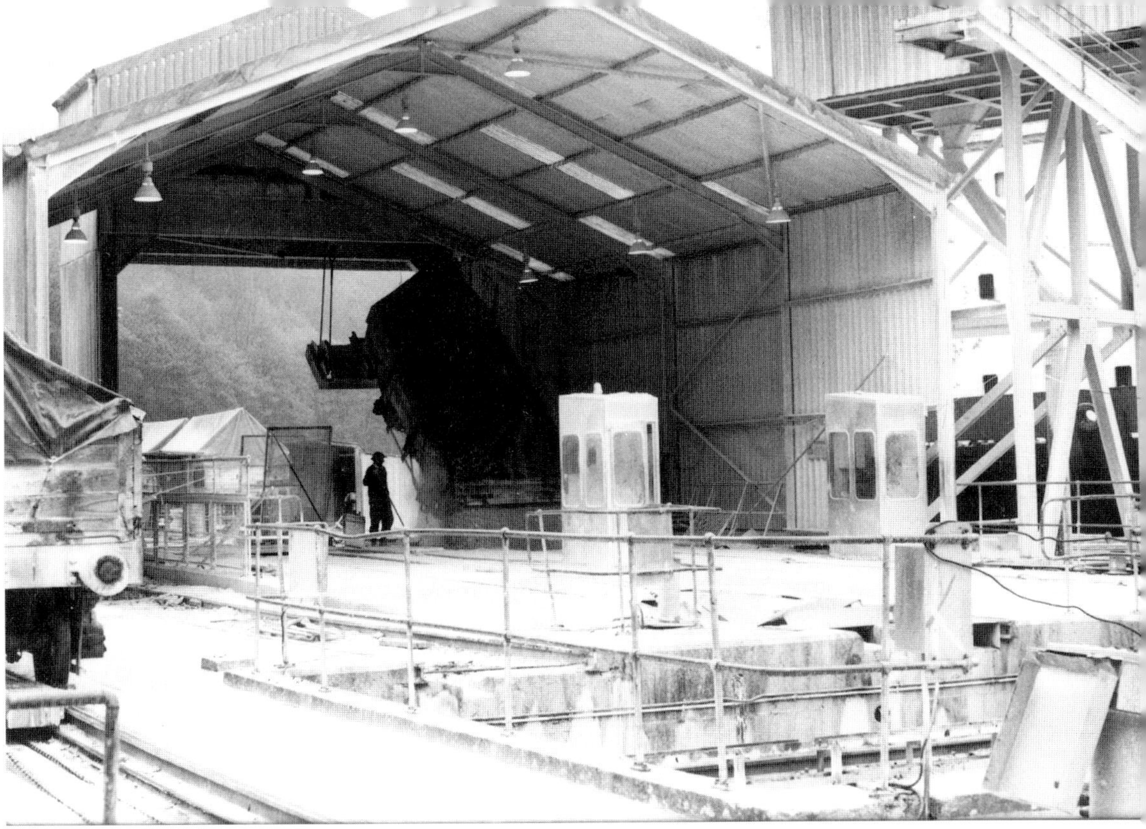

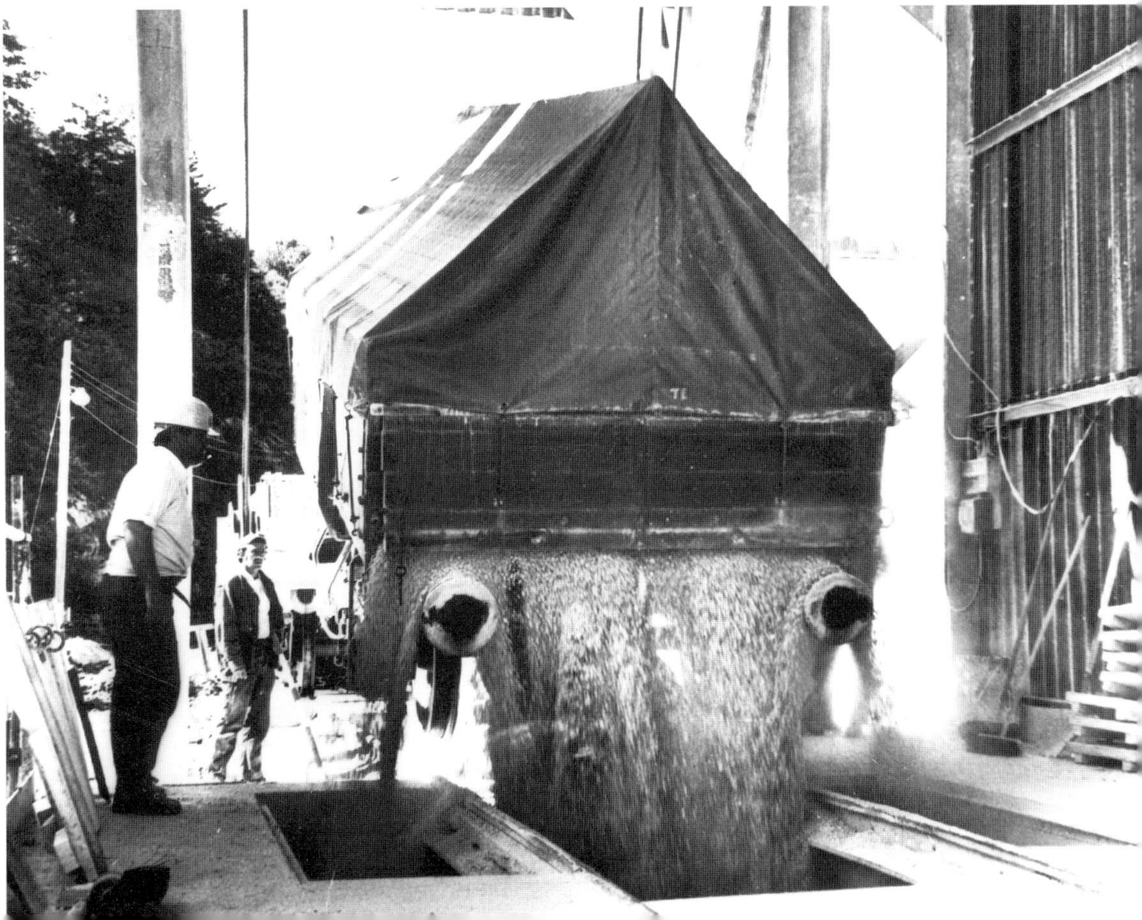

97. Wagons are moved by the "beetle", which is linked by means of a chain to an electrically powered winch. It is capable of propelling over 400 tons of clay. (P.G.Barnes)

98. The following four pictures were all taken in 1997. A close view of the electronic weighbridge shows the short length of rail which allows each axle to be weighed in transit. The door locks on the wagons are released automatically by the device in the background. (V.Mitchell)

99. While the "beetle" deals with the train, the shunter waves for more wagons to be propelled into position. The air braked CDA wagons carry 32 tonnes each, compared with 12 tons in the vacuum braked "clay hoods". The changeover took place during February 1988. (D.Mitchell)

Mineral tons per annum (1000s)	
1903	390
1913	559
1923	664
1933	573
1937	730
1948	337
1956	558
1996	800

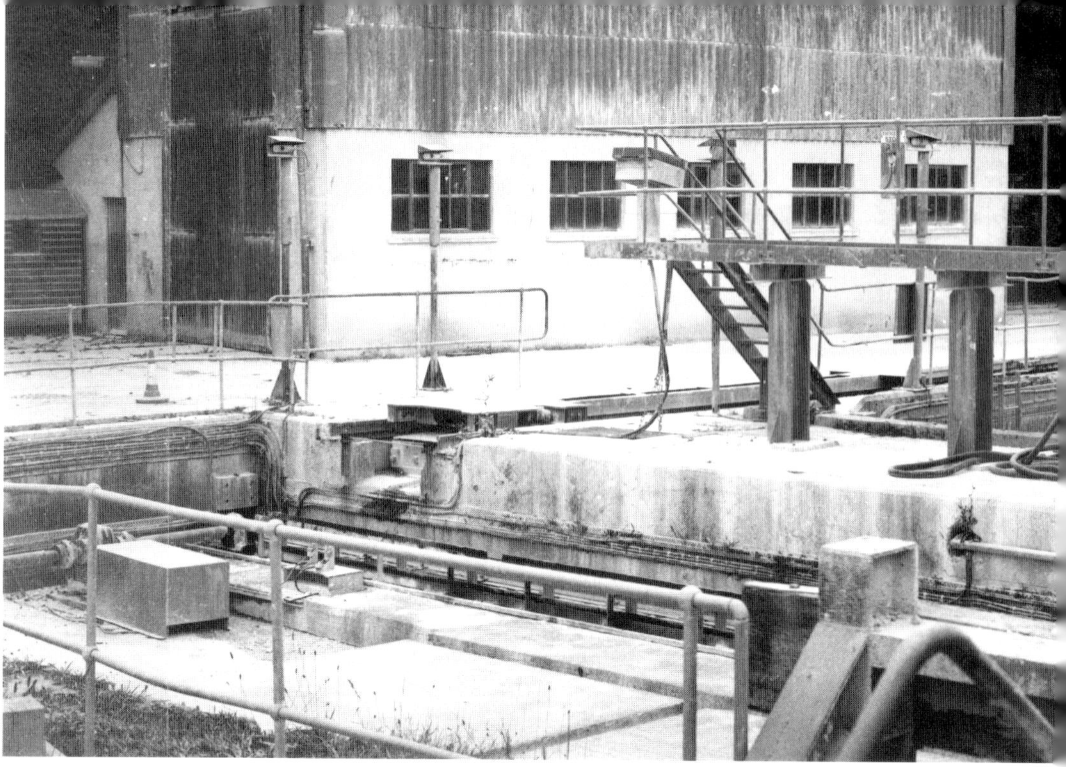

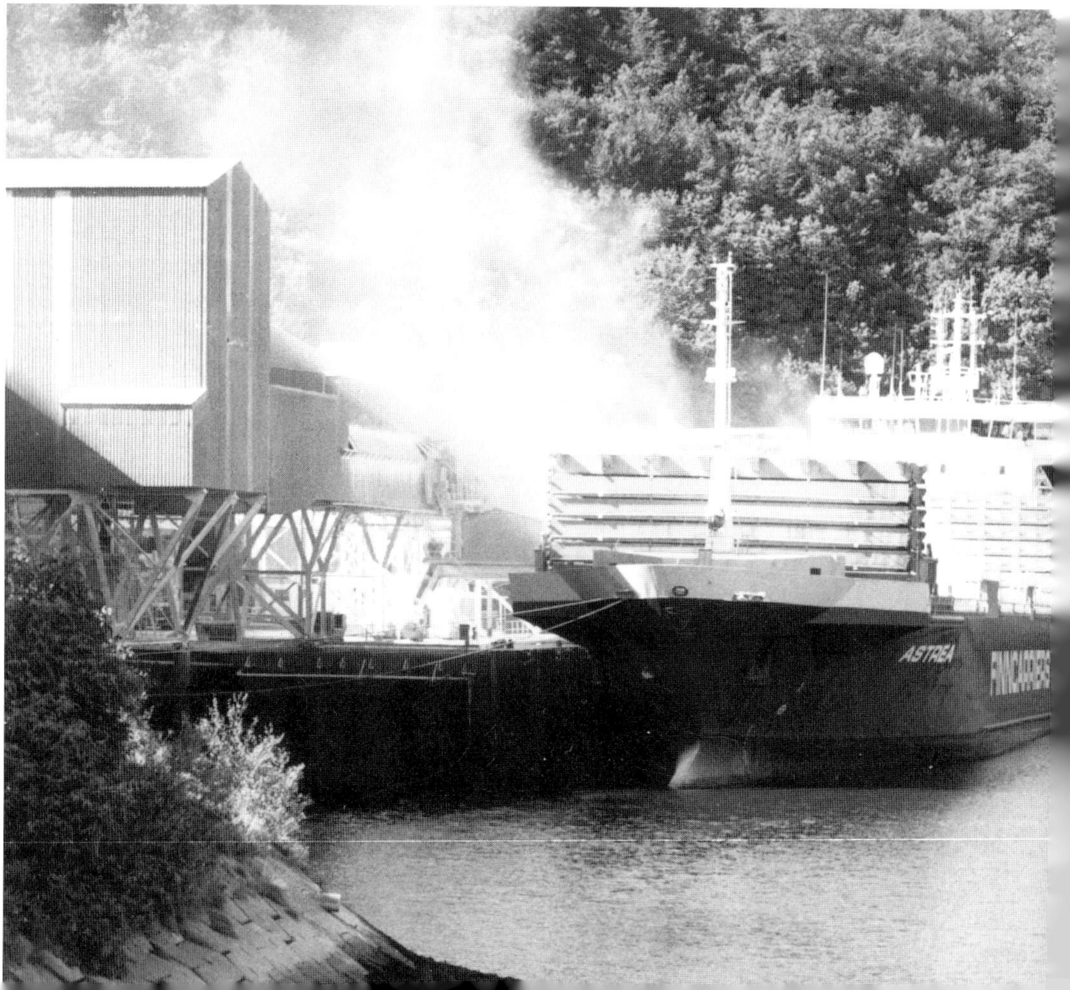
ASTREA

100. The modern wagons discharge through bottom doors. One wagon is being unloaded and the other is waiting to be unloaded. When this is complete they will be allowed to roll under gravity onto the two traversers. They will move to the left and depart on parallel sidings. The van is standing outside the former ECC engine shed. (V.Mitchell)

101. A cloud of clay dust rises from the hold of the *MV Astrea* as it is loaded, while no. 08576 stands with its barrier wagon, an HAA coal wagon. The end of labour restrictions in 1989 meant the staffing was reduced from 104 to 22 to ship the same tonnage. About 87% of the china clay produced in Cornwall is exported and some 300 grades are available. The major markets are in Western Europe, Scandinavia being the most important. Clay for export is normally despatched through the ports of Par (30%) and Fowey (70%). Clay for the United Kingdom market is distributed equally between road and rail. A single ship can be loaded with 11000 tonnes at this location; only two other jetties were in use by 1997. This is all private property and cannot be explored. (V.Mitchell)

FOWEY

102. Few photographs show all three platforms. Only the centre one was available in the CMR era, the GWR adding the one on the left when the Lostwithiel passenger service commenced in 1895. (M.Dart coll.)

103. The station and the line to St. Blazey are on the left, the ferry from Bodinnick is in the centre and on the right is no. 1 jetty. Behind it is the power station built by ECC in 1920 to supply the jetties. The nearby incline carried a siding to the generators. (M.Dart coll.)

Fowey	1903	1913	1923	1933
Passenger tickets issued	45237	51995	59544	33875
Season tickets issued	*	*	59	116
Parcels forwarded	12383	22388	16419	19060
General goods forwarded (tons)	1523	1927	1261	1129
Coal and coke received (tons)	92	231	412	78
General goods received (tons)	1830	2812	3132	2407
Trucks of livestock handled	-	3	5	9

(* not available)

104. Looking east from the footbridge in 1921, we observe no. 1259 shunting empty wagons. A new building stands on the site of the old loco/goods shed. A fresh shed was built in the goods yard. (K.Nunn/LCGB)

105. Class 5700 0-6-0PT no. 7716 is shunting on 22nd May 1935. The platform line on the left became a siding on 23rd August 1936, when buffer stops were erected at its west end. The line was removed on 18th March 1951. (H.C.Casserley)

106. Class 3581 2-4-0T no. 3582 waits with an autocoach in the abandoned platform on 7th June 1949. The roofless bridge was still standing, although last used by a passenger (officially) in 1936. (R.J.Buckley/C.Stacey)

107. There was no trace of the third line by the time that 0-4-2T no. 1419 was pictured in the mid-1950s. The post that once carried a gas light now has electric equipment with overhead wiring. The station was closed during the war from 1st January 1940 until 9th February 1942. The replacement bus service called at Torfrey Cross Roads for Golant. Only the station house (right) remained in 1997. (D.Lawrence)

108. An 0-4-2T propels its autocoach towards Lostwithiel on 13th August 1956 and runs alongside the retaining wall that supported the power station siding until it was lifted in 1965. (H.Davies)

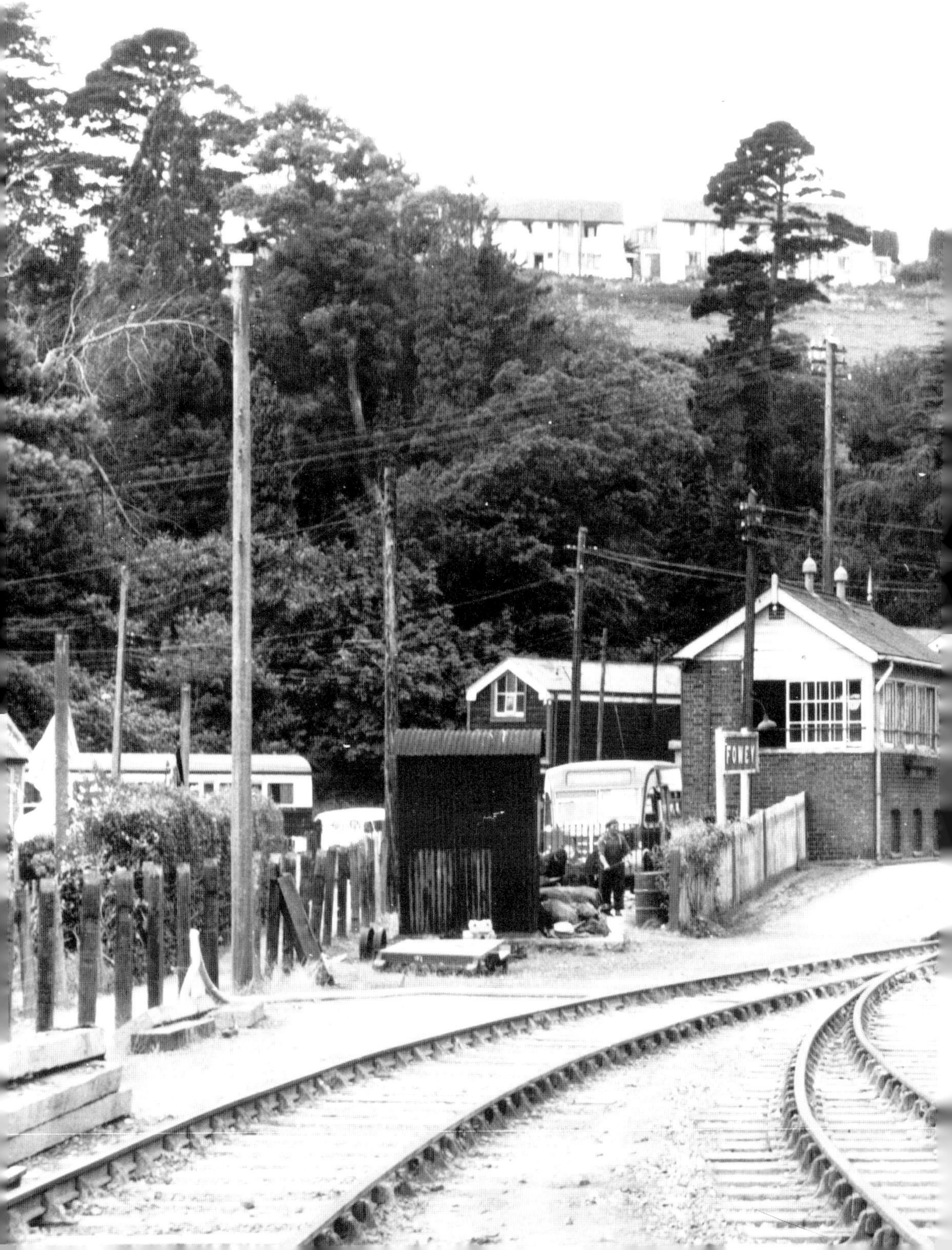
FOWEY

109. No. 8733 has just arrived from St. Blazey on 22nd July 1960 and waits to be called forward to the jetties. Don't miss the camping coach, the Bedford OB bus, the auto train and the 6-ton crane. The signal box was in use from 1895 until 1968. (R.C.Riley)

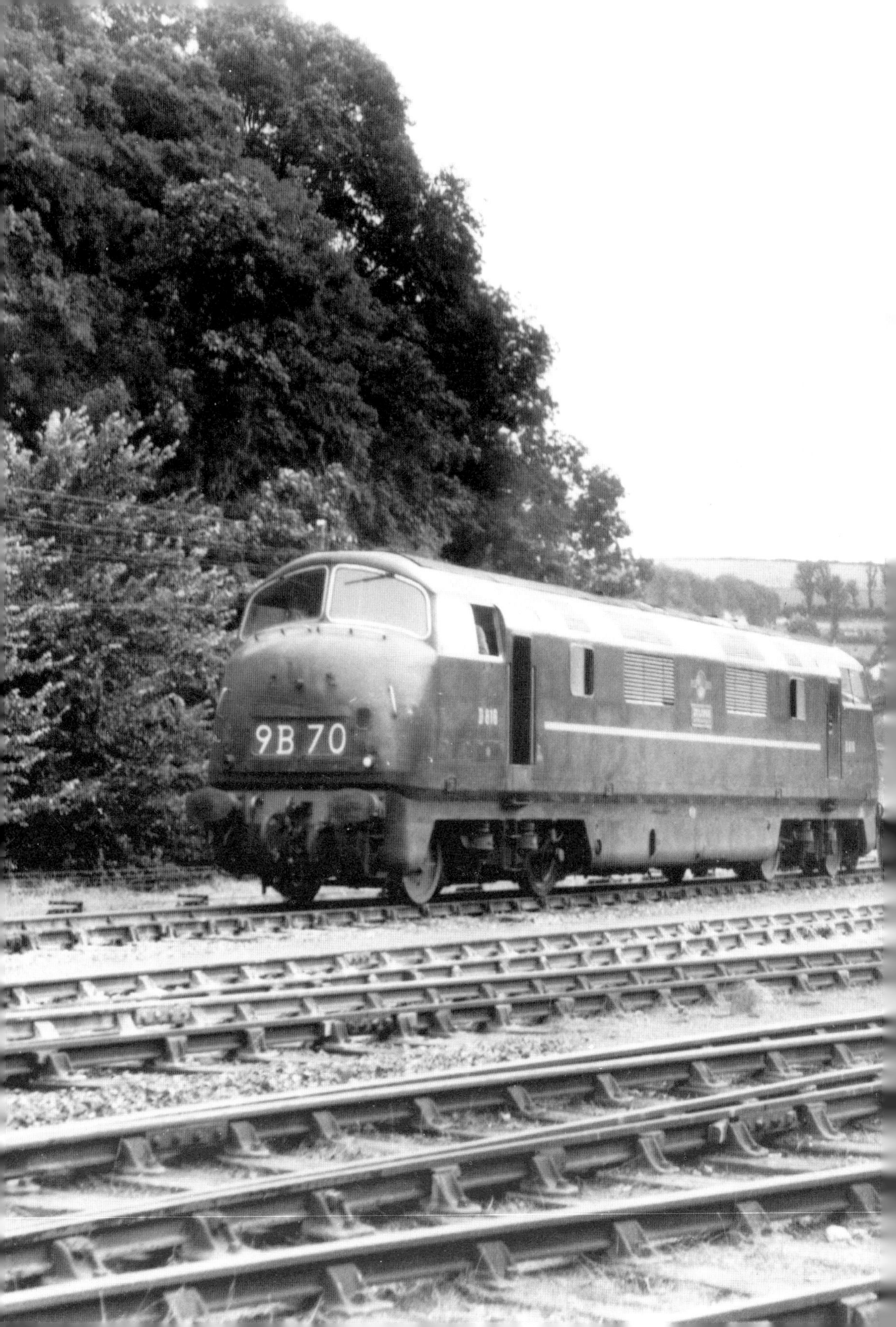
9B70

110. The goods yard was originally on the far side of the station, this one being laid out in about 1910. The goods shed followed after 1912. Public freight facilities were withdrawn on 1st June 1964. No. D816 *Eclipse* is leaving for St. Blazey with empties on 22nd July 1960. The "Warship" class had been introduced to the area in 1958. No. 1419 has been shunted clear of the running lines as it rests before its next journey to Lostwithiel. (R.C.Riley)

111. Class 4575 no. 5572 is recessed in the bay with its autocoach on 23rd September 1960 to leave the through lines clear. Class 4200 2-8-0T no. 4273 is arriving with loaded clay wagons from St. Blazey. Fowey had a population of a little over 2000 when passenger services were withdrawn on 4th January 1965. (R.C.Riley)

WEST OF FOWEY

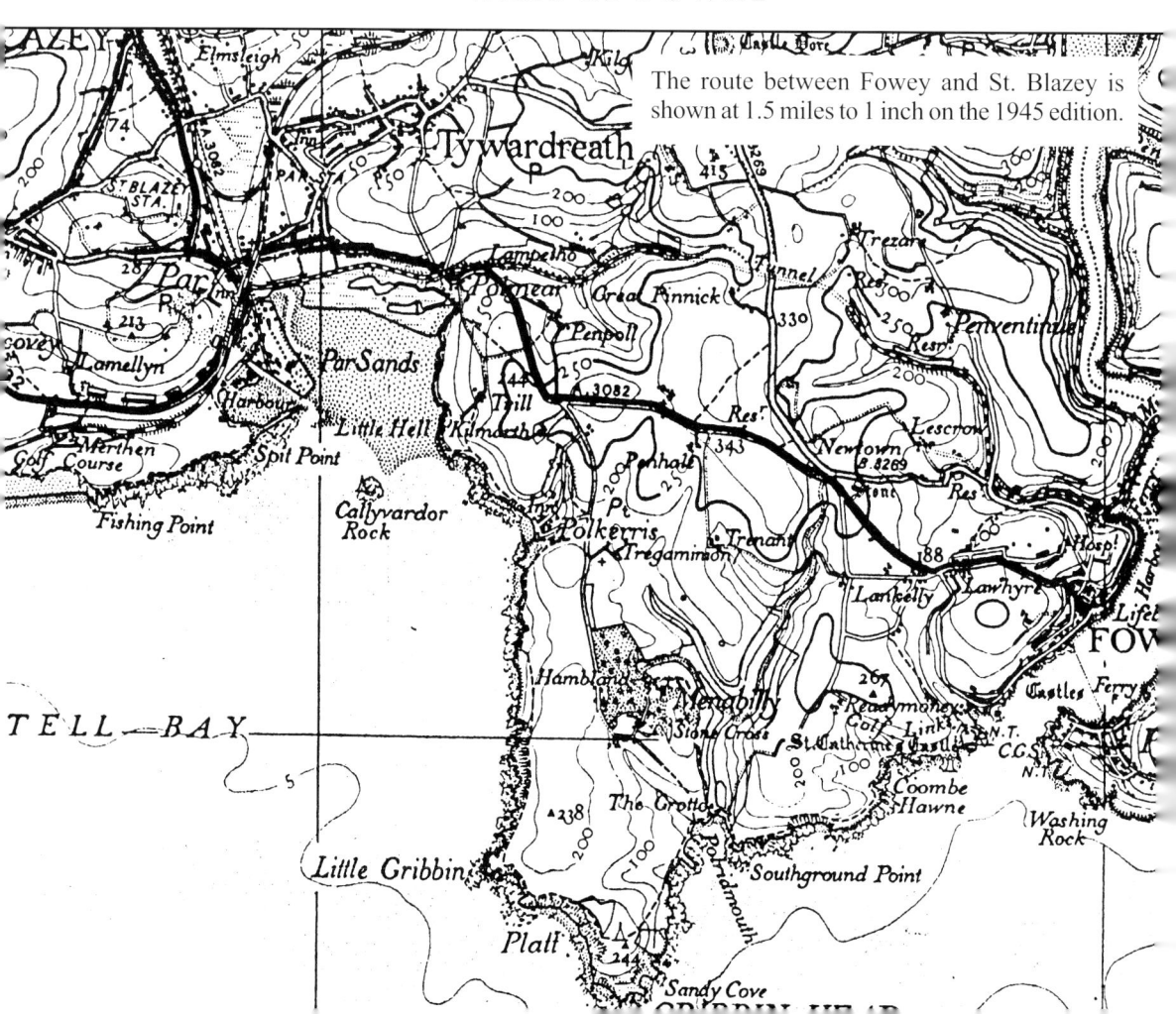

The route between Fowey and St. Blazey is shown at 1.5 miles to 1 inch on the 1945 edition.

112. The climb to the 1173yd long Pinnock Tunnel from Fowey was at 1 in 40. The east portal is seen from a 2-8-0T in 1960, as it reaches the short level length at the summit. (R.C.Riley)

113. The box was situated just behind the camera used for the previous picture. The box was in intermittent use between about 1907 and 1958. The tablet holders are obvious but the catcher is less clear; one is centre stage in picture 102. (M.Dart)

114. After closure in August 1968, the trackbed was converted into a private road by ECC and used by lorries between Par Harbour and Fowey Jetties. Largely unlined, Pinnock Tunnel has a steady inflow of water, although some extra lining was added. There was only one ventilation shaft and that was 100 yds from the east end, near a clapper gong that warned crews of the imminent sharp change of gradient. (ECC)

115. The construction of the haul road required 18000 tons of hardcore to widen the embankments and 15000 tons of tarmacadam for surfacing. Doors at the west end can be closed at weekends to allow suction fans (seen above the portal) to clear diesel fumes. Note the loading gauge and traffic lights. St. Blazey shed water reservoir is hidden by the building. (N.Langridge)

116. St. Blazey shed was usually allocated two of these 2-8-0Ts to work this difficult section of route. No. 4273 is facing the steep descent of 1 in 50 to Par Sands on 23rd September 1960 and has stopped as demanded by the sign. (R.C.Riley)

117. Further down the incline, the valley widens and presents splendid vistas. The crew of no. D816 will have had a more pleasant journey through Pinnock Tunnel than those choking and gasping on a 2-8-0T. (R.C.Riley)

118. We now approach Polmear, with Tywardreath in the background, and the crew of no. 4247 will have Par Sands in view. The date is 8th July 1955. Loaded trains were run via Golant as far as possible, this difficult route being used predominantly for empties. (R.C.Riley)

119. It was about 8pm when 2-8-0T no. 4247 was recorded on the near level track at Par Sands as it ran towards St. Blazey on 10th July 1957. The tennis players in this recreational area were not interested. (M.Dart)

ST. BLAZEY

120. Having turned from running westwards to northwards, we have joined the CMR original route from Par Harbour and have passed under the Penzance main line. We are crossing over the A3082 as the massive water tank of the locomotive depot comes into view. This was the base for most of the locomotives seen in the second half of this volume and will be featured in a forthcoming album. (R.C.Riley)

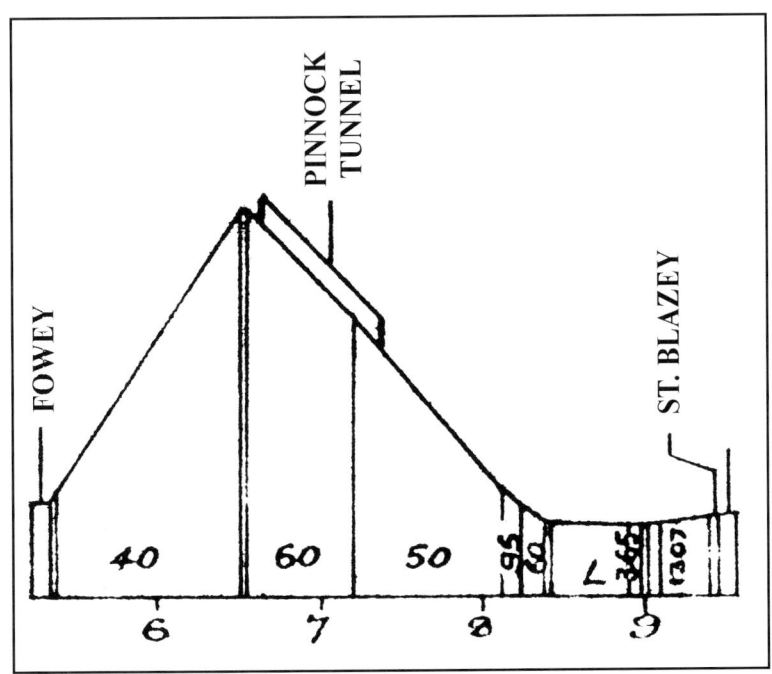

MP Middleton Press

Easebourne Lane, Midhurst, West Sussex. GU29 9AZ Tel: 01730 813169 Fax: 01730 812601
... WRITE OR PHONE FOR OUR LATEST LIST ...

BRANCH LINES
Branch Line to Allhallows
Branch Lines to Alton
Branch Lines around Ascot
Branch Line to Ashburton
Branch Lines around Bodmin
Branch Line to Bude
Branch Lines around Canterbury
Branch Line to Cheddar
Branch Lines to East Grinstead
Branch Lines to Effingham Junction
Branch Line to Fairford
Branch Line to Hawkhurst
Branch Line to Hayling
Branch Lines to Horsham
Branch Line to Ilfracombe
Branch Lines to Longmoor
Branch Line to Lyme Regis
Branch Line to Lynton
Branch Lines around Midhurst
Branch Line to Minehead
Branch Lines to Newport (IOW)
Branch Line to Padstow
Branch Lines around Plymouth
Branch Lines around Portmadoc 1923-46
Branch Lines around Porthmadog 1954-94
Branch Lines to Seaton & Sidmouth
Branch Line to Selsey
Branch Lines around Sheerness
Branch Line to Southwold
Branch Line to Swanage
Branch Line to Tenterden
Branch Lines to Torrington
Branch Line to Upwell
Branch Lines around Wimborne
Branch Lines around Wisbech

SOUTH COAST RAILWAYS
Ashford to Dover
Brighton to Eastbourne
Chichester to Portsmouth
Dover to Ramsgate
Portsmouth to Southampton
Ryde to Ventnor
Worthing to Chichester

SOUTHERN MAIN LINES
Bromley South to Rochester
Charing Cross to Orpington
Crawley to Littlehampton
Dartford to Sittingbourne
East Croydon to Three Bridges
Epsom to Horsham
Exeter to Barnstaple
Exeter to Tavistock
Faversham to Dover
Haywards Heath to Seaford
London Bridge to East Croydon
Orpington to Tonbridge
Sittingbourne to Ramsgate
Swanley to Ashford
Tavistock to Plymouth
Victoria to East Croydon
Waterloo to Windsor
Waterloo to Woking

Woking to Portsmouth
Woking to Southampton
Yeovil to Exeter

COUNTRY RAILWAY ROUTES
Bath to Evercreech Junction
Bournemouth to Evercreech Jn.
Burnham to Evercreech Junction
Croydon to East Grinstead
East Kent Light Railway
Fareham to Salisbury
Frome to Bristol
Guildford to Redhill
Porthmadog to Blaenau
Reading to Basingstoke
Reading to Guildford
Redhill to Ashford
Salisbury to Westbury
Strood to Paddock Wood
Taunton to Barnstaple
Westbury to Bath
Woking to Alton
Yeovil to Dorchester

GREAT RAILWAY ERAS
Ashford from Steam to Eurostar
Clapham Junction - 50 years of change
Festiniog in the Fifties
Festiniog in the Sixties

LONDON SUBURBAN RAILWAYS
Caterham and Tattenham Corner
Clapham Jn. to Beckenham Jn.
Crystal Palace and Catford Loop
East London Line
Finsbury Park to Alexandra Palace
Holborn Viaduct to Lewisham
Kingston and Hounslow Loops
Lines around Wimbledon
London Bridge to Addiscombe
Mitcham Junction Lines
North London Line
South London Line
West Croydon to Epsom
West London Line
Willesden Junction to Richmond
Wimbledon to Epsom

STEAM PHOTOGRAPHERS
O.J.Morris's Southern Railways 1919-59

STEAMING THROUGH
Steaming through Cornwall
Steaming through East Sussex
Steaming through the Isle of Wight
Steaming through Kent
Steaming through West Hants
Steaming through West Sussex

TRAMWAY CLASSICS
Aldgate & Stepney Tramways
Barnet & Finchley Tramways
Bath Tramways
Bournemouth & Poole Tramways

Brighton's Tramways
Bristol's Tramways
Camberwell & W.Norwood Tramways
Croydon's Tramways
Clapham & Streatham Tramways
Dover's Tramways
East Ham & West Ham Tramways
Eltham & Woolwich Tramways
Embankment & Waterloo Tramways
Enfield & Wood Green Tramways
Exeter & Taunton Tramways
Gosport & Horndean Tramways
Greenwich & Dartford Tramways
Hampstead & Highgate Tramways
Hastings Tramways
Holborn & Finsbury Tramways
Ilford & Barking Tramways
Kingston & Wimbledon Tramways
Lewisham & Catford Tramways
Liverpool Tramways 1. Eastern Routes
Maidstone & Chatham Tramways
North Kent Tramways
Portsmouth's Tramways
Reading Tramways
Seaton & Eastbourne Tramways
Southampton Tramways
Southend-on-sea Tramways
Southwark & Deptford Tramways
Stamford Hill Tramways
Thanet's Tramways
Victoria & Lambeth Tramways
Walthamstow & Leyton Tramways
Wandsworth & Battersea Tramways

TROLLEYBUS CLASSICS
Croydon's Trolleybuses
Hastings Trolleybuses
Maidstone Trolleybuses
Reading Trolleybuses
Woolwich & Dartford Trolleybuses

WATERWAY ALBUMS
Kent and East Sussex Waterways
London's Lost Route to the Sea
London to Portsmouth Waterway
Surrey Waterways

MILITARY BOOKS
Battle over Sussex 1940
Blitz over Sussex 1941-42
Bombers over Sussex 1943-45
Bognor at War
Military Defence of West Sussex
Secret Sussex Resistance

OTHER BOOKS
Betwixt Petersfield & Midhurst
Brickmaking in Sussex
Garraway Father & Son
Index to all Stations
London Chatham & Dover Railway

SOUTHERN RAILWAY VIDEO
War on the Line